Originally published as two volumes: *The Edda*
Vol. I: The Divine Mythology of the North
&
Vol. II: The Heroic Mythology of the North
© Winifred Faraday, 1902.
© Sign of the Phœnix, 1902.

This edition: *The Edda: The Divine & Heroic Mythology of the North*
© Finis Mundi Press, 2011.

Proofreader: Robert Ledwidge

Finis Mundi Press
http:/finismundipress.blogspot.com

ISBN: 978-989-8336-28-6
Copyright deposit: 334527/11

A record copy of this book is available at the
Portuguese National Library.

Finis Mundi is a registered trademark of Antagonista Editora (Portugal)

The Edda: The Divine & Heroic Mythology of the North

by
Winifred Faraday

Finis Mundi Press

Contents

Author's Note • 7

I - The Divine Mythology of the North • 9

II - The Heroic Mythology of the North • 45

III – Bibliography • 91

Supplement

Paganism as a *Weltanschauung* • 93
by Ramón Bau

Winifred Faraday

Author's Note

Some explanation is needed of the form of spelling I have adopted in transcribing Norse proper names. The spirants *þ* and *ð* are represented by *th* and *d*, as being more familiar to readers unacquainted with the original. Marks of vowel-length are in all cases omitted. The inflexional *-r* of the nominative singular masculine is also omitted, whether it appears as *-r* or is assimilated to a preceding consonant (as in Odinn, Eysteinn, Heindall, Egill) in the Norse form, with the single exception of the name Tyr, where I use the form which has become conventional in English.

Winifred Faraday
Manchester,
December 1901.

Winifred Faraday

I
The Divine Mythology of the North

The Icelandic Eddas are the only vernacular record of Germanic heathendom as it developed during the four centuries which in England saw the destruction of nearly all traces of the heathen system. The so-called Elder Edda is a collection of some thirty poems, mythic and heroic in substance, interspersed with short pieces of prose, which survives in a thirteenth-century MS., known as the Codex Regius, discovered in Iceland in 1642; to these are added other poems of similar character from other sources. The Younger Edda is a prose paraphrase of, and commentary on, these poems and others which are lost, together with a treatise on metre, written by the historian Snorri Sturluson about 1220.

This use of the word Edda is incorrect and unhistorical, though convenient and sanctioned by the use of several centuries. It was early used as a general term for the rules and materials for versemaking, and applied in this sense to Snorri's work. When the poems on which his paraphrase is founded were discovered, Icelandic scholars by a misunderstanding applied the name to them also; and as they attributed the collection quite arbitrarily to the historian Saemund (1056–1133), it was long known as Saemundar Edda, a name now generally discarded in favour of the less misleading titles of Elder or Poetic Edda. From its application to this collection, the word derives a more extended use, (1) as a general term for Norse mythology; (2) as a convenient name to distinguish the simpler style of these anonymous narrative poems from the elaborate formality of the Skalds.[1]

The poems of the Edda are certainly older than the MS., although the old opinion as to their high antiquity is untenable. The majority probably dates from the tenth century in their present form; this dating does not necessitate the ascription of the shape in which the legends are presented, still less of their substance, to that period. With regard to the place of their composition opinions vary widely, Norway, the British Isles and Greenland having all found champions; but the evidence is rather questionable, and I incline to leave them to the country which has preserved them. They are possibly of popular origin; this, together with their epic or narrative character, would account for the striking absence from them of some of the chief characteristics of Skaldic poetry: the obscuring of the sense by the elaborate interlacing of sentences and the extensive use of kennings or mythological synonyms, and the complication of the metre by such expedients as the conjunction of end-rhyme with alliteration. Eddic verse is governed solely by the latter, and the strophic arrangement is simple, only two forms occurring: (1) couplets of

---

[1] The chief apologists for the British theory are Professor Bugge (*Studien über die Entstehung der nordischen Götter- und Heldensagen*, München, 1889), and the editors of the *Corpus Poeticum Boreale* (see the Introduction to that work, and also the Prolegomena prefixed to their edition of the *Sturlunga Saga*, Oxford). The case for Norway and Greenland is argued by Dr. Finnur Jónsson (*Den oldnorsk og oldislandske Literaturs-Historie*, Copenhagen). The cases for both British and Norwegian origin are based chiefly on rather fanciful arguments from supposed local colour. The theory of the *Corpus Poeticum* editors that many of the poems were composed in the Scottish isles is discredited by the absence of Gaelic words or traces of Gaelic legend. Professor Bugge's North of England theory is slightly stronger, being supported by several Old English expressions in the poems, but these are not enough to prove that they were composed in England, since most Icelanders travelled east at some time of their lives.

alliterative short lines; (2) six-line strophes, consisting of a couplet followed by a single short line, the whole repeated.[2]

Roughly speaking, the first two-fifths of the MS. is mythological, the rest heroic. I propose to observe this distinction, and to deal in this study with the stories of the Gods. In this connexion, Snorri's Edda and the mythical Ynglinga Saga may also be considered, but as both were compiled a couple of centuries or more after the introduction of Christianity into Iceland, it is uncertain how much in them is literary explanation of tradition whose meaning was forgotten; some also, especially in Snorri, is probably pure invention, fairy tale rather than myth.

Many attempts have been made to prove that the material of the Edda is largely borrowed. The strength and distinction of Icelandic poetry rest rather on the fact that it is original and national and, like that of Greece, owes little to foreign sources; and that it began in the heathen age, before Christian or Romantic influences had touched Iceland. Valuable as the early Christian poetry of England is, we look in vain there for the humour, the large-minded simplicity of motive, the suggestive character-drawing, the swift dramatic action, which are as conspicuous in many poems in the Edda as in many of the Sagas.

Omitting the heroic poems, there are in Codex Regius the following: (1) Of a more or less comprehensive character, *Völuspa, Vafthrudnismal, Grimnismal, Lokasenna, Harbardsljod*; (2) dealing

---

[2]*Ynglinga Saga* is prefixed to the Lives of the Kings in the collection known as *Heimskringla* (edited by Unger, Christiania, 1868, and by Finnur Jónsson, Christiania, 1893); there is an English translation in Laing's *Lives of the Kings of Norway* (London, 1889).

with episodes, *Hymiskvida, Thrymskvida, Skirnisför. Havamal* is a collection of proverbs, but contains two interpolations from mythical poems; *Alvissmal*, which, in the form of a dialogue between Thor and a dwarf Alviss, gives a list of synonyms, is a kind of mythologico-poetical glossary. Several of these poems are found in another thirteenth-century vellum fragment, with an additional one, variously styled *Vegtamskvida* or *Baldr's Dreams*; the great fourteenth-century codex Flateybook contains *Hyndluljod*, partly genealogical, partly an imitation of *Völuspa*; and one of the MSS. of Snorri's Edda gives us *Rigsthula*.[3]

Völuspa, though not one of the earliest poems, forms an appropriate opening. Metrical considerations forbid an earlier date than the first quarter of the eleventh century, and the last few lines are still later. The material is, however, older: the poem is an outline, in allusions often obscure to us, of traditions and beliefs familiar to its first hearers. The very bareness of the outline is sufficient proof that the material is not new. The framework is apparently imitated from that of the poem known as *Baldr's Dreams*, some lines from which are inserted in *Völuspa*. This older poem describes Odin's visit to the Sibyl in hell-gates to inquire into the future. He rides down to her tomb at the eastern door of Nifl-hell and chants spells, until she awakes and asks: "What man unknown to me is that, who has troubled me with this weary journey? Snow has snowed on me, rain has beaten me, dew has drenched me, I have long been dead." He gives the name Wegtam, or Way-wise, and then follow question and

---

[3]A poem of similar form occurs among the heroic poems. *Gripisspa*, a prophetic outline of Sigurd's life, introduces the Volsung poems, as *Völuspa* does the Asgard cycle.

answer until she discovers his identity and will say no more. In *Völuspa* there is no descriptive introduction, and no dialogue; the whole is spoken by the Sibyl, who plunges at once into her story, with only the explanatory words: "Thou, Valfather, wouldst have me tell the ancient histories of men as far as I remember." She describes the creation of the world and sky by Bor's sons; the building by the Gods of a citadel in Ida-plain, and their age of innocence till three giant-maids brought greed of gold; the creation of the dwarfs; the creation of the first man and woman out of two trees by Odin, Hoeni and Lodur; the world-ash and the spring beside it where dwell the three Norns who order the fates of men. Then follows an allusion to the war between the Aesir and the Vanir, the battle with the giants who had got possession of the goddess Freyja, and the breaking of bargains; an obscure reference to Mimi's spring where Odin left his eye as a pledge; and an enumeration of his war-maids or Valkyries. Turning to the future, the Sibyl prophesies the death of Baldr[4], the vengeance on his slayer, and the chaining of Loki, the doom of the Gods and the destruction of the world at the coming of the fire-giants and the release of Loki's children from captivity. The rest of the poem seems to be later; it tells how the earth shall rise again from the deep, and the Aesir dwell once more in Odin's halls, and there is a

---

[4] The Baldr theories are stated in the following authorities: (1) Ritual origin: Frazer, *The Golden Bough*, vol. 3; (2) Heroic origin: Golther, *Handbuch der Germanischen Mythologie* (Leipzig, 1895); Niedner, *Eddische Fragen* (*Zeitschrift für deutsches Altertum*, new series, 29), *Zur Lieder-Edda* (*Zeitschr. f. d. Alt.* Vol. 36); (3) Solar myth: Sir G.W. Cox, *Mythology of the Aryan Nations* (London, 1870); Max Müller, *Chips from a German Workshop*, vol. 4; (4) Borrowed: Bugge, *Studien über die Entstehung der nordischen Götter- und Heldensagen* (transl. Brenner, München, 1889).

suggestion of Christian influence in it which is absent from the earlier part.[5]

Of the other general poems, the next four were probably composed before 950; in each the setting is different. *Vafthrudnismal*, a riddle-poem, shows Odin in a favourite position, seeking in disguise for knowledge of the future. Under the name of Gangrad (Wanderer), he visits the wise giant Vafthrudni, and the two agree to test their wisdom: the one who fails to answer a question is to forfeit his head. In each case the questions deal first with the past. Vafthrudni asks about Day and Night, and the river which divides the Giants from the Gods, matters of common knowledge; and then puts a question as to the future: "What is the aplain where Surt and the blessed Gods shall meet in battle?" Odin replies, and proceeds to question in his turn; first about the creation of Earth and Sky, the origin of Sun and Moon, Winter and Summer, the Giants and the Winds; the coming of Njörd the Wane to the Aesir as a hostage; the Einherjar, or chosen warriors of Valhalla. Then come prophetic questions on the destruction of the Sun by the wolf Fenri, the Gods who shall rule in the new world after Ragnarök, the end of Odin. The poem is brought to a close by Odin's putting the question which only himself can answer: "What did Odin say in his son's ear before he mounted the pyre?" and the giant's head is forfeit.

In the third poem of this class, *Grimnismal*, a prose introduction relates that Odin and Frigg quarrelled over the merits of their respective foster-children. To settle the question, Odin goes disguised

---

[5] So many of the mythological poems are in this form that they suggest the question, did the asking of riddles form any part of Scandinavian ritual?

as Grimni, "the Hooded One," to visit his foster-son Geirröd; but Frigg, to justify her charge of inhospitality against Geirröd, sends her maiden Fulla to warn him against the coming stranger. Odin therefore meets with a harsh reception, and is bound between two fires in the hall. Geirröd's young son, Agnar, protests against this rude treatment, and gives wine to the guest, who then begins to instruct him in matters concerning the Gods. He names the halls of the Aesir, describes Valhalla and the ash Yggdrasil, the Valkyries, the creation of the world (two stanzas in common with *Vafthrudnismal*), and enumerates his own names. The poem ends with impressive abruptness by his turning to Geirröd:

"Thou art drunk, Geirröd, thou hast drunk too deep; thou art bereft of much since thou hast lost my favour, the favour of Odin and all the Einherjar. I have told thee much, but thou hast minded little. Thy friends betray thee: I see my friend's sword lie drenched in blood. Now shall Odin have the sword-weary slain; I know thy life is ended, the Fates are ungracious. Now thou canst see Odin: come near me, if thou canst."

[Prose.] "King Geirröd sat with his sword on his knee, half drawn. When he heard that Odin was there, he stood up and would have led Odin from the fires. The sword slipt from his hand; the hilt turned downwards. The king caught his foot and fell forwards, the sword standing towards him, and so he met his death. Then Odin went away, and Agnar was king there long afterwards."

Harbardsljod is a dialogue, and humorous. Thor on his return from the east comes to a channel, at the farther side of which stands Odin, disguised as a ferryman, Greybeard. He refuses to ferry Thor across, and they question each other as to their past feats, with occasional threats from Thor and taunts from Odin, until the former goes off vowing vengeance on the ferryman:

Thor. "Thy skill in words would serve thee ill if I waded across the water; I think thou wouldst cry louder than the wolf, if thou shouldst get a blow from the hammer."

Odin. "Sif has a lover at home, thou shouldst seek him. That is a task for thee to try, it is more proper for thee."

Thor. "Thou speakest what thou knowest most displeasing to me; thou cowardly fellow, I think that thou liest."

Odin. "I think I speak true; thou art slow on the road. Thou wouldst have got far, if thou hadst started at dawn."

Thor. "Harbard, scoundrel, it is rather thou who hast delayed me."

Odin. "I never thought a shepherd could so delay Asa-Thor's journey."

Thor. "I will counsel thee: row thy boat hither. Let us cease quarrelling; come and meet Magni's father."

Odin. "Leave thou the river; crossing shall be refused thee."

Thor. "Show me the way, since thou wilt not ferry me."

Odin. "That is a small thing to refuse. It is a long way to go: a while to the stock, and another to the stone, then keep to the left hand till thou reach Verland. There will Fjörgyn meet her son Thor, and she will tell him the highway to Odin's land."

Thor. "Shall I get there to-day?"

Odin. "With toil and trouble thou wilt get there about sunrise, as I think."

Thor. "Our talk shall be short, since thou answerest with mockery. I will reward thee for refusing passage, if we two meet again."

Odin. "Go thy way, where all the fiends may take thee."

Lokasenna also is in dialogue form. A prose introduction tells how the giant Oegi, or Gymi, gave a feast to the Aesir. Loki was turned out for killing a servant, but presently returned and began to revile the Gods and Goddesses, each one in turn trying to interfere, only to provoke a taunt from Loki. At last Thor, who had been absent on a journey, came in and threatened the slanderer with his hammer, whereupon Loki said, "I spoke to the Aesir and the sons of the Aesir what my mind told me; but for thee alone I will go away, for I know thou wilt strike." Some of the poem is rather pointless abuse, but much touches points already suggested in the other poems.

Hyndluljod is much later than the others, probably not before 1200. The style is late, and the form imitated from *Völuspa*. It describes a visit paid by Freyja to the Sibyl to learn the genealogy of her favourite Ottar. The larger part deals with heroic genealogies, but there are scanty allusions to Baldr, Frey, Heimdal, Loki's children, and Thor, and a Christian reference to a God who shall come after Ragnarök "when Odin shall meet the wolf." It tells nothing new.

We have here then, omitting *Hyndluljod*, five poems (four of them belonging to the first half of the tenth century) which suggest a general outline of Norse mythology: there is a hierarchy of Gods, the Aesir, who live together in a citadel, Odin being the chief. Among them are several who are not Aesir by origin: Njörd and his son and daughter, Frey and Freyja, are Vanir; Loki is really an enemy and an agent in their fall; and there are one or two Goddesses of giant race. The giants are rivals and enemies to the Gods; the dwarfs are also antagonistic, but in bondage. The meeting-place of the Gods is by the World-Ash, Yggdrasil, on whose well-being the fate of Gods and men depends; at its root lies the World-Snake. The Gods have foreknowledge of their own doom, Ragnarök, the great fight when they shall meet Loki's children, the Wolf and the Snake; both sides will fall and the world be destroyed. An episode in the story is the death of Baldr. This we may assume to be the religion of the Viking age (800–1000 A.D.), a compound of the beliefs of various ages and tribes.[6]

The Aesir.—The number of the Aesir is not fixed. *Hyndluljod* says there were twelve ("there were eleven Aesir when Baldr went down into the howe"). Snorri gives a list of fourteen Aesir or Gods (Odin, Thor, Baldr, Njörd, Frey, Tyr, Bragi, Heimdal, Höd, Vidar, Vali, Ullr, Forseti, Loki), and adds Hoeni in another list, all the fifteen occurring in the poems; and sixteen Goddesses (Asynjor), the majority of whom are merely personified epithets, occurring nowhere else. Of the sixteen, Frigg, Gefion, Freyja and Saga (really an epithet only) are Goddesses in the poems, and Fulla is Frigg's handmaid. In another chapter, Snorri adds Idunn, Gerd, Sigyn and Nanna, of whom the latter does not appear in the Elder Edda, where Idunn, Gerd (a giantess) and Sigyn are the wives of Bragi, Frey and Loki; and two others, the giantess Skadi and Sif, are the wives of Njörd and Thor.

---

[6]*Ynglinga Saga* says that Odin and the Aesir came to Norway from Asia; a statement due, of course, to a false etymology, though theories as to the origin of Norse mythology have been based on it.

A striking difference from classical mythology is that neither Tyr[7] (who should etymologically be the Sky-god), nor Thor (the Thunder-god), takes the highest place. Tyr is the hero of one important episode, the chaining of the Wolf, through which he loses his right hand. This is told in full by Snorri and alluded to in *Lokasenna*, both in the prose preface ("Tyr also was there, with only one hand; the Fenris-wolf had bitten off the other, when he was bound") and in the poem itself:

Loki. "I must remember that right hand which Fenri bit off thee."

Tyr. "I am short of a hand, but thou of the famous wolf; to each the loss is ill-luck. Nor is the wolf in better plight, for he must wait in bonds till Ragnarök."

Otherwise, he only appears in connexion with two more popular Gods: he speaks in Frey's defence in *Lokasenna*, and in *Hymiskvida* he is Thor's companion in the search for a cauldron; the latter poem represents him as a giant's son.

Thor, on the other hand, is second only to his father Odin; he is the strongest of the Gods and their champion against the giants, and his antagonist at Ragnarök is to be the World-Snake. Like Odin, he travels much, but while the chief God generally goes craftily and in disguise, to gain knowledge or test his wisdom, Thor's errands are warlike; in *Lokasenna* he is absent on a journey, in *Harbardsljod* and *Alvissmal* he is returning from one. His journeys are always to the east; so in *Harbardsljod*: "I was in the east, fighting the malevolent giant-brides.... I was in the east and guarding the river, when

---

[7] Tyr is etymologically identical with Zeus, and with the Sanskrit Dyaus (Sky-God).

Svarang's sons attacked me." The Giants live in the east (*Hymiskvida* 5); Thor threatened Loki: "I will fling thee up into the east, and no one shall see thee more" (*Lokasenna* 59); the fire-giants at Ragnarök are to come from the east: "Hrym comes driving from the east, he lifts his shield before him.... A ship comes from the east, Muspell's sons will come sailing over the sea, and Loki steers" (*Völuspa* 50, 51). It would not, perhaps, be overstraining the point to suggest that this is a reminiscence of early warfare between the Scandinavians and eastern nations, either Lapps and Finns or Slavonic tribes.

Thor is the God of natural force, the son of Earth. Two of the episodical poems deal with his contests with the giants. *Thrymskvida*, the story of how Thor won back his hammer, Mjöllni, from the giant Thrym, is the finest and one of the oldest of the mythological poems; a translation is given in the appendix, as an example of Eddic poetry at its best. Loki appears as the willing helper of the Gods, and Thor's companion. The Thunderer's journey with Tyr in quest of a cauldron is related with much humour in *Hymiskvida*: Hymi's beautiful wife, who helps her guests to outwit her husband, is a figure familiar in fairy-tales as the Ogre's wife.

The chief God of the Scandinavians is, it must be confessed, an unsympathetic character. He is the head of the Valhalla system; he is Val-father (Father of the Slain), and the Valkyries are his "Wishmaidens," as the Einherjar are his "Wishsons." He naturally takes a special interest in mortal heroes, from whom come the chosen hosts of Valhalla. But, in spite of the splendour of his surroundings, he is wanting in dignity. The chief of the Gods has neither the might and unthinking valour of Thor, nor the self-sacrificing courage of Tyr. He is a God who practises magic, and it is as Father of Spells that he is powerful. He is the wisest of the Gods in the sense that he remembers most about the past and foresees most about the future; yet he is powerless in difficulty without the craft of Loki and the hammer of Thor. He always wanders in disguise, and the stories told of him are chiefly love-adventures; this is true of all the deeds he mentions in *Harbardsljod*, and also of the two interpolations in *Havamal*, though one of the two had an object, the stealing of the mead of inspiration from the giant Suptung, whose daughter Gunnlöd guarded it.

Völuspa makes him one of three creative deities, the other two being Lodur (probably Loki) and Hoeni, of whom nothing else is known except the story that he was given as hostage to the Vanir in exchange for Njörd. The same three Gods (Odin, Loki and Hoeni) are connected with the legend of the Nibelung treasure; and it was another adventure of theirs, according to Snorri, which led to the loss of Idunn.

Of the other Gods, Bragi is a later development; his name means simply king or chief, and his attributes, as God of eloquence and poetry, are apparently borrowed from Odin. Heimdal, the watchman and "far-seeing like the Vanir," who keeps guard on the rainbow bridge Bifröst, is represented in the curious poem *Rigsthula* as founder of the different social orders. He wandered over the world under the name of Rig, and from his first journey sprang the race of thralls, swarthy, crooked and broad-backed, who busied themselves with fencing land and tending goats and swine; from his second, the churls, fine and ruddy, who broke oxen, built houses and ploughed the land; from his third, the earls, yellow-haired, rosy, and keen-eyed, who broke horses and strung bows, rode, swam, and hurled spears; and the youngest of the earls' race was Konung the king, who knew all mysteries, understood the speech of birds, could quench fire and heal wounds. Heimdal is said to be the son of nine mothers, and to have fought with Loki for Freyja's Brising-necklace. His horn is hidden under Yggdrasil, to be brought out at Ragnarök, when he will blow a warning blast. His origin is obscure. Still less is known of Vidar and Vali, two sons of Odin, one of whom is to avenge Baldr's death, the other to slay the wolf after it has swallowed up the chief God at Ragnarök. Thor's stepson Ullr (Glory) is probably, like his sons Modi and Magni (Wrath and Strength), a mere epithet.

Frigg, Odin's wife and the chief Goddess, daughter of Earth, is not very distinctly characterised, and is often confused with Freyja. Gefion should be the sea-goddess, since that seems to be the meaning of her name, but her functions are apparently usurped by the Wane Njörd; according to Snorri, she is the patron of those who die unwedded.

Baldr.—The story of Baldr is the most debated point in the Edda. The chief theories advanced are: (1) That it is the oldest part of Norse mythology, and of ritual origin; (2) that Baldr is really a hero transformed into a God; (3) that the legend is a solar myth with or without Christian colouring; (4) that it is entirely borrowed from Mediæval Greek and Christian sources. This last theory is too ingenious to be credible; and with regard to the third, there is nothing essentially Christian in the chief features of the legend, while the solar idea leaves too much unexplained. The references to the myth in the Elder Edda are:

(1) *Vegtamskvida*[8] (about 900 A.D.). Odin questions the Sibyl as to the meaning of Baldr's dreams:

Odin. "For whom are the benches (in hell) strewn with rings, the halls fairly adorned with gold?"

Sibyl. "Here the mead, clear drink, stands brewed for Baldr; the shields are spread. The sons of the Aesir are too merry."

Odin. "Who will be Baldr's slayer and rob Odin's son of life?"

Sibyl. "Höd bears thither the high branch of fame: he will be Baldr's slayer and rob Odin's son of life."

Odin. "Who will avenge the deed on Höd and bring Baldr's slayer to the funeral pyre?"

Sibyl. "Rind bears a son, Vali, in the halls of the west. He shall not wash his hands nor comb his hair till he bears Baldr's foe to the pyre."

(2) In *Lokasenna* Frigg says: "If I had a son like Baldr here in Oegi's halls, thou shouldst not pass out from the sons of the Aesir, but be slain here in thy anger"; to which Loki replies, "Wilt thou that I speak more ill words, Frigg? I am the cause that thou wilt never more see Baldr ride into the hall."[9]

---

[8]The word *hroðrbaðm* (which I have given as "branch of fame") would perhaps be more accurately translated "tree of fame," which Gering explains as a kenning for Baldr. But there are no kennings of the same sort in the poem, and the line would have no meaning. If it refers to the mistletoe, as most commentators agree, it merely shows that the poet was ignorant of the nature of the plant, which would be in favour of its antiquity, rather than the reverse.

[9]English translation by Professor Elton (London, D. Nutt, 1894). As Saxo's references to the old Gods are made in much the same sympathetic tone as that adopted by Old Testament writers towards heathen deities, his testimony on mythological questions is of the less value.

(3) In *Vafthrudnismal* the only reference is Odin's question, "What said Odin in his son's ear when he mounted the pyre?"

(4) In *Völuspa* the Sibyl prophesies, "I saw doom threatening Baldr, the bleeding victim, the son of Odin. Grown high above the meadows stood the mistletoe, slender and fair. From this stem, which looked so slender, grew a fatal and dangerous shaft. Höd shot it, and Frigg wept in Fenhall over Valhall's woe." The following lines, on the chaining of Loki, suggest his complicity.

(5) *Hyndluljod* has one reference: "There were eleven Aesir by number when Baldr went down into the howe. Vali was his avenger and slew his brother's slayer."

Besides these there is a fragment quoted by Snorri: "Thökk will weep dry tears at Baldr's funeral pyre. I had no good of the old man's son alive or dead; let Hel keep what she has." *Grimnismal* assigns a hall to Baldr among the Gods.

There are, in addition, two prose versions of the story by later writers: the Icelandic version of Snorri (1178–1241) with all the details familiar to everyone; and the Latin one of the Dane Saxo Grammaticus (about thirty years earlier), which makes Baldr and Höd heroes instead of Gods, and completely alters the character of the legend by making a rivalry for Nanna's favour the centre of the plot and cause of the catastrophe. On the Eddic version and on Saxo's depend the theories of Golther, Detter, Niedner and other German scholars on the one hand, and Dr. Frazer on the other.

It has often been pointed out that there is no trace of Baldr-worship in other Germanic nations, nor in any of the Icelandic sagas except the late Frithjofssaga. This, however, is true of other Gods, notably of Tyr, who is without question one of the oldest. The only deities named with any suggestion of sacrifice or worship in the Icelandic sagas proper are Odin, Thor, Frey, Njörd, Frigg and Freyja. The process of choice is as arbitrary in mythology as in other sciences. Again, it is more likely that the original version of the legend should have survived in Iceland than in Denmark, which, being on the mainland, was earlier subject to Christian and Romantic influences; and that a heathen God should, in the two or three centuries following the establishment of Christianity in the North, be turned into a mortal hero, than that the reverse process should have acted at a sufficiently late date to permit of both versions existing side by side in the thirteenth century. A similar gradual elimination of the supernatural may be found in the history of the Volsung myth. Snorri's version is merely an amplification of that in the Elder Edda, which, scanty as its account of Baldr is, leaves no doubt as to his divinity.

The outline gathered from the poems is as follows: Baldr, Odin's son, is killed by his brother Höd through a mistletoe spray; Loki is in some way concerned in his death, which is an overwhelming misfortune to the Gods; but it is on Höd that his death is avenged. He is burnt on a pyre (Snorri says on his ship, a feature which must come from the Viking age; *Hyndluljod* substitutes howe-burial). He will be absent from the great fight at Ragnarök, but *Völuspa* adds that he will return afterwards. Nanna has nothing to do with the story. The connexion with the hierarchy of the Aesir seems external only, since Baldr has no apparent relation to the great catastrophe as have Odin, Thor, Frej, Tyr and Loki; this, then, would point to the independence of his myth.

The genuineness of the myth seems to depend on whether the mistletoe is an original feature of it or not, and on this point there can be little real doubt. The German theory that Baldr could only be killed by his own sword, which was therefore disguised by enchantment and used against him, and that the Icelandic writers misunderstood this to mean a mistletoe sprig, is far-fetched and romantic, and crumbles at a touch. For if, as it is claimed, the Icelanders had no mistletoe, why should they introduce it into a story to which it did not belong? They might preserve it by tradition, but they would hardly invent it. Granting this, the mistletoe becomes the central point of the legend. The older mythologists, who only saw in it a sun-myth, overlooked the fact that since any weapon would have done to kill the God with, the mistletoe must have some special significance; and if it is a genuine part of the story, as we have no reason to doubt, it will be hard to overturn Dr. Frazer's theory that the Baldr-myth is a relic of tree-worship and the ritual sacrifice of the God, Baldr being a tree-spirit whose soul is contained in the mistletoe[10].

The contradictions in the story, especially as told by Snorri (such as the confusion between the parts played by Höd and Loki, and the unsuspicious attitude of the Gods as Loki directs Höd's aim) are sometimes urged against its genuineness. They are rather proofs of antiquity. Apparent contradictions whose explanation is forgotten

---

[10]It seems incredible that any writers should turn to the travesty of the Baldr story given in the almost worthless saga of Hromund Gripsson in support of a theory. In it "Bildr" is killed by Hromund, who has the sword Mistilteinn. It must be patent to any one that this is a perverted version of a story which the narrator no longer understood.

often survive in tradition; the inventor of a new story takes care to make it consistent. It is probable, however, that there were originally only two actors in the episode, the victim and the slayer, and that Loki's part is later than Höd's, for he really belongs to the Valhall and Ragnarök myth, and was only introduced here as a link. The incident of the oath extracted from everything on earth to protect Baldr, which occurs in Snorri and in a paper MS. of *Baldr's Dreams*, was probably invented to explain the choice of weapon, which would certainly need explanation to an Icelandic audience. If Dr. Frazer's theory be right, Vali, who slew the slayer, must also have been an original figure in the legend. His antiquity is supported by the fact that he plays the part of avenger in the poems; while in Snorri, where he is mentioned as a God, his absence from the account of Baldr's death is only a part of that literary development by which real responsibility for the murder was transferred from Höd to Loki.

Snorri gives Baldr a son, Forseti (Judge), who is also named as a God in *Grimnismal*. He must have grown out of an epithet of Baldr's, of whom Snorri says that "no one can resist his sentence"; the sacred tree would naturally be the seat of judgment.

* * * * *

The Wanes.—Three of the Norse divinities, Njörd and his son and daughter, are not Aesir by descent. The following account is given of their presence in Asgard:

(1) In *Vafthrudnismal*, Odin asks:

"Whence came Njörd among the sons of the Aesir? for he was not born of the Aesir."

Vafthrudni. "In Vanaheim wise powers ordained and gave him for a hostage to the Gods; at the doom of the world he shall come back, home to the wise Wanes."

(2) There is an allusion in *Völuspa* to the war which caused the giving of hostages:

"Odin shot into the host: this was the first war in the world. Broken was the wall of the citadel of the Aesir, so that the Wanes could tread the fields of war."

(3) Loki[11] taunts Njörd with his position, in *Lokasenna*:

"Thou wast sent from the east as a hostage to the Gods...."

Njörd. "This is my comfort, though I was sent from far as a hostage to the Gods, yet I have a son whom no one hates, and he is thought the best of the Aesir."

Loki. "Stay, Njörd, restrain thy pride; I will hide it no longer: thy son is thine own sister's son, and that is no worse than one would expect."

Tyr. "Frey is the best of all the bold riders of Asgard."

There is little doubt that Njörd was once a God of higher importance than he is in the Edda, where he is overshadowed by his son. Grimm's suggestion that he and the goddess Nerthus, mentioned by Tacitus, were brother and sister, is supported by the line in *Lokasenna*; it is an isolated reference, and the Goddess has left no other traces in Scandinavian mythology. They were the deities,

---

[11]It is hardly necessary to point out the parallel between Loki and Prometheus, also both helper and enemy of the Gods, and agent in their threatened fall, though in the meantime a prisoner. In character Loki has more in common with the mischievous spirit described by Hesiod, than with the heroic figure of Aeschylus. The struggles of Loki (p. 28) find a parallel in those of the fire-serpent Typhon, to which the Greeks attributed earthquakes.

probably agricultural, of an earlier age, whose adoption by the later Northmen was explained by the story of the compact between Aesir and Vanir. Then their places were usurped by Frey and Freyja, who were possibly created out of epithets originally applied to the older pair; Njörd was retained with lessened importance, Nerthus passed out altogether. The Edda gives Njörd a giant-bride, Skadi, who was admitted among the Gods in atonement for the slaying of her father Thiazi; she is little more than a name. Frey and Freyja have other marks of agricultural deities, besides their relationship. Nothing is said about Frey's changing shape, but Freyja possesses a hawk-dress which Loki borrows when he wishes to change his form; and, according to Snorri, Frey was sacrificed to for the crops. Njörd has an epithet, "the wealthy," which may have survived from his earlier connexion with the soil. In that case, it would explain why, in Snorri and elsewhere, he is God of the sea and ships, once the province of the ocean-goddess Gefion; the transference is a natural one to an age whose wealth came from the sea.

In spite of their origin, Frey and Freyja become to all intents and purposes Aesir. Frey is to be one of the chief combatants at Ragnarök, with the fire-giant Surt for his antagonist, and a story is told to explain his defeat: he fell in love with Gerd, a giant-maid, and sacrificed his sword to get her; hence he is weaponless at the last fight. Loki alludes to this episode in *Lokasenna*: "With gold didst thou buy Gymi's daughter, and gavest thy sword for her; but when Muspell's sons ride over Myrkwood, thou shalt not know with what to fight, unhappy one." The story is told in full in *Skirnisför*.

Freyja is called by Snorri "the chief Goddess after Frigg," and the two are sometimes confused. Like her father and brother, she comes into connexion with the giants; she is the beautiful Goddess, and coveted by them. *Völuspa* says that the Gods went into consultation to discuss "who had given the bride of Od (*i.e.*, Freyja) to the giant race"; *Thrymskvida* relates how the giant Thrym bargained for Freyja as the ransom for Thor's hammer, which he had hidden, and how Loki and Thor outwitted him; and Snorri says the giants bargained for her as the price for building Valhalla, but were outwitted. Sir G.W. Dasent notices in the folk-tales the eagerness of trolls and giants to learn the details of the agricultural processes, and this is probably the clue to the desire of the Frost-Giants in the Edda for the possession of Freyja. Idunn, the wife of Bragi, and a purely Norse creation, seems to be a double of Freyja; she, too, according to Snorri, is carried away by the giants and rescued by Loki. The golden apples which she is to keep till Ragnarök remind us of those which Frey offered to Gerd; and the gift of eternal youth, of which they are the symbols, would be appropriate enough to Freyja as an agricultural deity.

The great necklace Brising, stolen by Loki and won back in fight by Heimdal (according to the tenth-century Skalds Thjodulf and Ulf Uggason), is Freyja's property. On this ground, she has been identified with the heroine of *Svipdag and Menglad*, a poem undoubtedly old, though it has only come down in paper MSS. It is in two parts, the first telling how Svipdag aroused the Sibyl Groa, his mother, to give him spells to guard him on his journey; the second describing his crossing the wall of fire which surrounded his fated bride Menglad. If Menglad is really Freyja, the "Necklace-glad," it is a curious coincidence that one poem connects the waverlowe, or ring of fire, with Frey also; for his bride Gerd is protected in the same way, though his servant Skirni goes through it in his place:

Skirni. "Give me the horse that will bear me through the dark magic waverlowe, and the sword that fights of itself against the giant-race."

Frey. "I give thee the horse that will bear thee through the dark magic waverlowe, and the sword that will fight of itself if he is bold who bears it." (*Skirnisför.*)

The connexion of both with the Midsummer fires, originally part of an agricultural ritual, can hardly be doubted.

* * * * *

Loki, or Lopt, is a strange figure. He is admitted among the Aesir, though not one of them by birth, and his whole relation to them points to his being an older elemental God. He is in alliance with them against the giants; he and Odin have sworn blood-brothership, according to *Lokasenna*, and he helps Thor to recover his hammer that Asgard may be defended against the giants. On the other hand, while in present alliance with the Gods, he is chief agent in their future destruction, and this they know. In Snorri, he is a mischievous spirit of the fairy-tale kind, exercising his ingenuity alternately in getting the Gods into difficulties, and in getting them out again. So he betrays Idunn to the giants, and delivers her; he makes the bargain by which Freyja is promised to the giant-builders of Valhalla, and invents the trick by which they are cheated of their prize; by killing the otter he endangers his own head, Odin's and Hoeni's, and he obtains the gold which buys their atonement. Hence, in the systematising of the Viking religion, the responsibility for Baldr's death also was transferred to him. At the coming of the fire-giants at Ragnarök, he is to steer the ship in which Muspell's sons sail (*Völuspa*), further evidence of his identity as a fire-spirit. Like his son the Wolf, he is chained by the Gods; the episode is related in a prose-piece affixed to *Lokasenna*:

"After that Loki hid himself in Franangr's Foss in the form of a salmon. There the Aesir caught him. He was bound with the guts of his son Nari, but his son Narfi was changed into a wolf. Skadi took a poisonous snake and fastened it up over Loki's face, and the poison dropped down. Sigyn, Loki's wife, sat there and held a cup under the poison. But when it was full she poured the poison away, and meanwhile poison dropped on Loki, and he struggled so hard that all the earth shook; those are called earthquakes now."

Völuspa inserts lines corresponding to this passage after the Baldr episode, and Snorri makes it a consequence of Loki's share in that event.

He is more especially agent of the doom through his children: at Ragnarök, Fenri the Wolf, bound long before by Tyr's help, will be freed, and swallow the sun (*Vafthrudnismal*) and Odin (*Vafthrudnismal* and *Völuspa*); and Jörmungandr, the Giant-Snake, will rise from the sea where he lies curled round the world, to slay and be slain by Thor. The dragon's writhing in the waves is one of the tokens to herald Ragnarök, and his battle with Thor is the fiercest combat of that day. Only *Völuspa* of our poems gives any account of it: "Then comes the glorious son of Hlodyn, Odin's son goes to meet the serpent; Midgard's guardian slays him in his rage, but scarcely can Earth's son reel back nine feet from the dragon."

When Thor goes fishing with the giant Hymi, he terrifies his companion by dragging the snake's head out of the sea, but he does not slay it; it must wait there till Ragnarök:

"The protector of men, the only slayer of the Serpent, baited his hook with the ox's head. The God-hated one who girds all lands from below swallowed the bait. Doughtily pulled mighty Thor the poison-streaked serpent up to the side; he struck down with his hammer the hideous head of the wolf's companion. The monster roared, the wilderness resounded, the old earth shuddered all through. The fish sank back into the sea. Gloomy was the giant when they rowed back, so that he spoke not a word."

There is nothing to suggest that Jörmungandr, to whom the word World-Snake (Midgardsorm) always refers in the Edda, is the same as Nidhögg, the serpent that gnaws at Yggdrasil's roots; but both are relics of Snake-worship.

* * * * *

The World-Ash, generally called Yggdrasil's Ash, is one of the most interesting survivals of tree-worship. It is described by the Sibyl in *Völuspa*: "I know an ash called Yggdrasil, a high tree sprinkled with white moisture (thence come the dews that fall in the dales): it stands ever-green by Urd's spring. Thence come three maids, all-knowing, from the hall that stands under the tree"; and as a sign of the approaching doom she says: "Yggdrasil's ash trembles as it stands;

the old tree groans." *Grimnismal* says that the Gods go every day to hold judgment by the ash, and describes it further:

"Three roots lie three ways under Yggdrasil's ash: Hel dwells under one, the frost-giants under the second, mortal men under the third. The squirrel is called Ratatosk who shall run over Yggdrasil's ash; he shall carry down the eagle's words, and tell them to Nidhögg below. There are four harts, with necks thrown back, who gnaw off the shoots.... More serpents lie under Yggdrasil's ash than any one knows. Ofni and Svafni I know will ever gnaw at the tree's twigs. Yggdrasil's ash suffers more hardships than men know: the hart bites above, the side decays, and Nidhögg gnaws below.... Yggdrasil's ash is the best of trees."

The snake and the tree are familiar in other mythologies, though in most other cases the snake is the protector, while here he is the destroyer. Both Nidhögg and Jörmungandr are examples of the destroying dragon rather than the treasure-guardian. The Ash is the oracle: the judgment-place of the Gods, the dwelling of the Fates, the source of the spring of knowledge. * * * * *

Ragnarök.—The Twilight of the Gods (or Doom of the Gods) is the central point of the Viking religion. The Regin (of which *Ragna* is genitive plural) are the ruling powers, often called Ginnregin (the great Gods), Uppregin (the high Gods), Thrymregin (the warrior Gods). The word is commonly used of the Aesir in *Völuspa*; in *Alvissmal* the Regin seem to be distinguished from both Aesir and Vanir. The whole story of the Aesir is overshadowed by knowledge of this coming doom, the time when they shall meet foes more terrible than the giants, and fall before them; their constant effort is to learn what will happen then, and to gather their forces together to meet it. The coming Ragnarök is the reason for the existence of Valhalla with its hosts of slain warriors; and of all the Gods, Odin, Thor, Tyr and Loki are most closely connected with it. Two poems of the verse Edda describe it:

(1) *Vafthrudnismal*:

V. "What is the plain called where Surt and the blessed Gods shall meet in battle?"

O. "Vigrid is the name of the place where Surt and the blessed Gods shall meet in battle. It is a hundred miles every way; it is their destined battle-field." * * * * *

O. "Whence shall the sun come on the smooth heaven when Fenri has destroyed this one?"

V. "Before Fenri destroy her, the elf-beam shall bear a daughter: that maid shall ride along her mother's paths, when the Gods perish."

O. "Which of the Aesir shall rule over the realms of the Gods, when Surt's fire is quenched?"

V. "Vidar and Vali shall dwell in the sanctuary of the Gods when Surt's fire is quenched. Modi and Magni shall have Mjöllni at the end of Vingni's (*i.e.*, Thor's) combat."

O. "What shall be Odin's end, when the Gods perish?"

V. "The Wolf will swallow the father of men; Vidar will avenge it. He will cleave the Wolf's cold jaws in the battle."

(2) *Völuspa*:

"A hag sits eastward in Ironwood and rears Fenri's children; one of them all, in troll's shape, shall be the sun's destroyer. He shall feed on the lives of death-doomed men; with red blood he shall redden the seat of the Gods. The sunshine shall grow black, all winds will be unfriendly in the after-summers.... I see further in the future the great Ragnarök of the Gods of Victory.... Heimdal blows loudly, the horn is on high; Yggdrasil's ash trembles as it stands, the old tree groans."

The following lines tell of the fire-giants and the various combats, and the last section of the poem deals with a new world when Baldr, Höd and Hoeni are to come back to the dwelling-place of the Gods.

The whole points to a belief in the early destruction of the world and the passing away of the old order of things. Whether the new world which *Vafthrudnismal* and *Völuspa* both prophesy belongs to the original idea or not is a disputed point. Probably it does not; at all events, none of the old Aesir, according to the poems, are to survive, for Modi and Magni are not really Gods at all, Baldr, Höd and Vali belong to another myth, Hoeni had passed out of the hierarchy by his exchange with Njörd, and Vidar's origin is obscure.

* * * * *

The Einherjar, the great champions or chosen warriors, are intimately connected with Ragnarök. All warriors who fall in battle are taken to Odin's hall of the slain, Valhalla. According to *Grimnismal*, he "chooses every day men dead by the sword"; his Valkyries ride to battle to give the victory and bring in the fallen. Hence Odin is the giver of victory. Loki in *Lokasenna* taunts him with giving victory to the wrong side: "Thou hast never known how to decide the battle among men. Thou hast often given victory to those to whom thou shouldst not give it, to the more cowardly"; this, no doubt, was in order to secure the best fighters for Valhalla. That the defeated side sometimes consoled themselves with this explanation of a notable warrior's fall is proved by the tenth-century dirge on Eirik Bloodaxe, where Sigmund the Volsung asks in Valhalla: "Why didst thou take the victory from him, if thou thoughtest him brave?" and Odin replies: "Because it is uncertain when the grey Wolf will come to the seat of the Gods." There are similar lines in Eyvind's dirge on Hakon the Good. In this way a host was collected ready for Ragnarök: for *Grimnismal* says: "There are five hundred doors and eighty in Valhalla; eight hundred Einherjar will go out from each door, when they go to fight the wolf." Meanwhile they fight and feast: "All the Einherjar in Odin's courts fight every day: they choose the slain and ride from the battle, and sit then in peace together" (*Vafthrudnismal,*) and the Valkyries bear ale to them *(Grimnismal).*

It is often too hastily assumed that the Norse Ragnarök with the dependant Valhalla system are in great part the outcome of Christian influence: of an imitation of the Christian Judgment Day and the Christian heaven respectively. Owing to the lateness of our material, it is, of course, impossible to decide how old the beliefs may be, but it is likely that the Valhalla idea only took form at the systematising of the mythology in the Viking age. The belief in another world for the dead is, however, by no means exclusively Christian, and a reference in *Grimnismal* suggests the older system out of which, under the influence of the Ragnarök idea, Valhalla was developed. The lines, "The ninth hall is Folkvang, where Freyja rules the ordering of seats in the hall; half the slain she chooses every day, Odin has the other half," are an evident survival of a belief that all the dead went to live with the Gods, Odin having the men, and Freyja (or more probably Frigg) the women; the idea being here confused with the later system, under which only those who fell in battle were chosen by the Gods. Christian colouring appears in the last lines of *Völuspa* and in Snorri, where men are divided into the "good and moral," who go after death to a hall of red gold, and the "perjurers and murderers," who are sent to a hall of snakes.

For Ragnarök also a heathen origin is at least as probable as a Christian one. I would suggest as a possibility that the expectation of the Twilight of the Gods may have grown out of some ritual connected with the eclipse, such as is frequent among heathen races. Such ceremonies are a tacit acknowledgment of a doubt, and if they ever existed among the Scandinavians, the possibility, ever present to the savage mind, of a time when his efforts to help the light might be fruitless, and the darkness prove the stronger, would be the germ of his more civilised descendant's belief in Ragnarök.[12]

By turning to the surviving poems of the Skalds[13], whose dates can be approximately reckoned from the sagas, we can fix an inferior limit for certain of the legends given above, placing them definitely in the heathen time. Reference has already been made to the

---

[12]Mr. Lang, in *Myth, Ritual, and Religion*, (London, 1887) gives examples of eclipse ritual. Grimm, in the *Teutonic Mythology*, vol. 2, quotes Finnish and Lithuanian myths about sun-devouring beasts, very similar to the Fenri myth.

[13]All the Skaldic verses will be found, with translations, in the *Corpus Poeticum*.

corroboration of the Valhalla belief supplied by the elegies on Eirik Bloodaxe and Hakon the Good. In the former (which is anonymous, but must have been written soon after 950, since it was composed, on Eirik's death, by his wife's orders), Odin commands the Einherjar and Valkyries to prepare for the reception of the slain Eirik and his host, since no one knows how soon the Gods will need to gather their forces together for the great contest. Eyvind's dirge on Hakon (who fell in 970) is an imitation of this: Odin sends two Valkyries to choose a king to enter his service in Valhalla; they find Hakon on the battlefield, and he is slain with many of his followers. Great preparation is made in Valhalla for his reception, and the poet ends by congratulating Hakon (who, though a Christian, having been educated in England, had not interfered with the heathen altars and sacrifices) on the toleration which has secured him such a welcome. A still earlier poet, Hornklofi, writing during the reign of Harald Fairhair (who died in 933), alludes to the slain as the property of "the one-eyed husband of Frigg."

Several Skalds mention legends of Thor: his fishing for the World-Snake is told by Bragi (who from his place in genealogies must have written before 900), and by Ulf Uggason and Eystein Valdason, both in the second half of the tenth century; and Thjodulf and Eilif (the former about 960, the latter a little later) tell tales of his fights with the giants. Turning to the other Gods, Egil Skallagrimsson (about 970) names Frey and Njörd as the givers of wealth; Bragi tells the story of Gefion's dragging the island of Zealand out of Lake Wener into the sea; and Ulf Uggason speaks of Heimdal's wrestling with Loki.

The legend of Idunn is told by Thjodulf much as Snorri tells it: Odin, Hoeni and Loki, while on a journey, kill and roast an ox. The giant Thiazi swoops down in eagle's shape and demands a share; Loki strikes the eagle, who flies off with him, releasing him only on condition that he will betray to the giants Idunn, "the care-healing maid who understands the renewal of youth." He does so, and the Gods, who grow old and withered for want of her apples, force him to go and bring her back to Asgard.

The poet of *Eiriksmal*, quoted above, alludes to the Baldr myth: Bragi, hearing the approach of Eirik and his host, asks "What is that thundering and tramping, as if Baldr were coming back to Odin's hall?" The funeral pyre of Baldr is described by Ulf Uggason: he is burnt on his ship, which is launched by a giantess, in the presence of Frey, Heimdal, Odin and the Valkyries.

Though heathen writers outside of Scandinavia are lacking, references to Germanic heathendom fortunately survive in several Continental Christian historians of earlier date than any of our Scandinavian sources. The evidence of these, though scanty, is corroborative, and the allusions are in striking agreement with the Edda stories in tone and character.

Odin (Wodanus) is always identified by these writers with the Roman Mercurius (whom Tacitus named as the chief German God). This identification occurs in the eighth-century Paulus Diaconus, and in Jonas of Bobbio (first half of the seventh century), and probably rests on Odin's character as a wandering God (Mercury being διάκτορος), his disguises, and his patronage of poetry and eloquence (as Mercury is λόγιος). Odin is not himself in general the conductor of dead souls (ψυχοπομπός), like the Roman God, his attendant Valkyries performing the office for him. The equation is only comprehensible on the presumption of the independence of Germanic mythology, and cannot be explained by transmission. For if Odin were in any degree an imitation of the Roman deity, other notable attributes of the latter would have been assigned to him: whereas in the Edda the thieving God (κλέπτης) is not Odin but Loki, and the founder of civilisation is Heimdal.

The legend of the origin of the Lombards given by Paulus Diaconus illustrates the relations of Odin and Frigg. The Vandals asked Wodan (Odin) to grant them victory over the Vinili; the latter made a similar prayer to Frea (Frigg), the wife of Wodan. She advised them to make their wives tie their hair round their faces like beards, and go with them to meet Wodan in the morning. They did so, and Wodan exclaimed, "Who are these *Long-beards*?" Then Frea said that having given the Vinili a name, he must give them the victory (as Helgi in the Edda claims a gift from Svava when she names him). As in *Grimnismal*, Odin and Frigg are represented as supporting rival claims, and Frigg gains the day for her favourites by superior cunning. This legend also shows Odin as the giver of victory.

Few heathen legends are told however by these early Christian writers, and the Gods are seldom called by their German names. An exception is the Frisian Fosite mentioned by Alcuin (who died 804) and by later writers; he is to be identified with the Norse Forseti, the son of (probably at first an epithet of) Baldr, but no legend of him is told. It is disappointing that these writers should have said so little of any God except the chief one. A very characteristic touch survives in

Gregory of Tours (died 594), when the Frank Chlodvig tells his Christian wife that the Christian God "cannot be proved to be of the race of the Gods," an idea entirely in keeping with the Eddic hierarchy. Before leaving the Continental historians, reference may be made to the abundant evidence of Germanic tree-worship to be gathered from them. The holy oak mentioned by Wilibald (before 786), the sacred pear-tree of Constantius (473), with numerous others, supply parallels to the World-Ash which is so important a feature of Norse mythology.

A study of this subject would be incomplete without some reference to the mythology of Saxo Grammaticus. His testimony on the old religion is unwilling, and his effort to discredit it very evident. The bitterness of his attack on Frigg especially suggests that she was, among the Northmen, a formidable rival to the Virgin. When he repeats a legend of the Gods, he transforms them into mortal heroes, and when, as often happens, he refers to them accidentally as Gods, he invariably hastens to protest that he does so only because it had been the custom. He describes Thor and Odin as men versed in sorcery who claimed the rank of Gods; and in another passage he speaks of the latter as a king who had his seat at Upsala, and who was falsely credited with divinity throughout Europe. His description of Odin agrees with that in the Edda: an old man of great stature and mighty in battle, one-eyed, wearing a great cloak, and constantly wandering about in disguise. The story which Saxo tells of his driving into battle with Harald War-tooth, disguised as the latter's charioteer Brun, and turning the fight against him by revealing to his enemy Ring the order of battle which he had invented for Harald's advantage, is in thorough agreement with the traditional character of the God who betrayed Sigmund the Volsung and Helgi Hundingsbane. Saxo's version of the Baldr story has been mentioned already. Baldr's transformation into a hero (who could only be slain by a sword in the keeping of a wood-satyr) is almost complete. But Odin and Thor and all the Gods fight for him against his rival Hother, "so that it might be called a battle of Gods against men"; and Nanna's excuse to Baldr that "a God could not wed with a mortal," preserves a trace of his origin. The chained Loki appears in Saxo as Utgarda-Loki, lying bound in a cavern of snakes, and worshipped as a God by the Danish king Gorm Haraldsson. Dr. Eydberg sees the Freyja myth in Saxo's story of Syritha, who was carried away by the giants and delivered by her lover Othar (the Od of the Edda): an example, like *Svipdag and Menglad*, of the complete transformation of a divine into an heroic myth. In almost all cases Saxo vulgarises the stories in the telling, a common result when a mythical tale is retold by a Christian writer, though it is still more conspicuous in his versions of the heroic legends.

Winifred Faraday

II

The Heroic Mythology of the North

Sigemund the Waelsing and Fitela, Aetla, Eormanric the Goth and Gifica of Burgundy, Ongendtheow and Theodric, Heorrenda and the Heodenings, and Weland the Smith: all these heroes of Germanic legend were known to the writers of our earliest English literature. But in most cases the only evidence of this knowledge is a word, a name, here and there, with no hint of the story attached. For circumstances directed the poetical gifts of the Saxons in England towards legends of the saints and Biblical paraphrase, away from the native heroes of the race; while later events completed the exclusion of Germanic legend from our literature, by substituting French and Celtic romance. Nevertheless, these few brief references in *Beowulf* and in the small group of heathen English relics give us the right to a peculiar interest in the hero-poems of the Edda. In studying these heroic poems, therefore, we are confronted by problems entirely different in character from those which have to be considered in connexion with the mythical texts. Those are in the main the product of one, the Northern, branch of the Germanic race, as we have seen (No. 12 of this series), and the chief question to be determined is whether they represent, however altered in form, a mythology common to all the Germans, and as such necessarily early; or whether they are in substance, as well as in form, a specific creation of the Scandinavians, and therefore late and secondary. The heroic poems of the Edda, on the contrary, with the exception of the Helgi cycle, have very close analogues in the literatures of the other great

45

branches of the Germanic race, and these we are able to compare with the Northern versions.

The Edda contains poems belonging to the following heroic cycles:

(*a*) **Weland the Smith.**—Anglo-Saxon literature has several references to this cycle, which must have been a very popular one; and there is also a late Continental German version preserved in an Icelandic translation. But the poem in the Edda is the oldest connected form of the story.

(*b*) **Sigurd and the Nibelungs.**—Again the oldest reference is in Anglo-Saxon. There are two well-known Continental German versions in the *Nibelungen Lied* and the late Icelandic *Thidreks Saga*, but the Edda, on the whole, has preserved an earlier form of the legend. With it is loosely connected

(*c*) **The Ermanric Cycle.**—The oldest references to this are in Latin and Anglo-Saxon. The Continental German version in the *Thidreks Saga* is late, and, like that in the Edda, contaminated with the Sigurd story, with which it had originally nothing to do.

(*d*) **Helgi.**—This cycle, at least in its present form, is peculiar to the Scandinavian North.

All the above-named poems are contained in Codex Regius of the Elder Edda. From other sources we may add other poems which are Eddic, not Skaldic, in style, in which other heroic cycles are represented. The great majority of the poems deal with the favourite story of the Volsungs, which threatens to swamp all the rest; for one hero after another, Burgundian, Hun, Goth, was absorbed into it. The poems in this part of the MS. differ far more widely in date and style than do the mythological ones; many of the Volsung-lays are comparatively late, and lack the fine simplicity which characterises the older popular poetry.

Völund.—The lay of Völund[14], the wonderful smith, the Weland of the Old English poems and the only Germanic hero who survived for any considerable time in English popular tradition, stands alone in its cycle, and is the first heroic poem in the MS. It is in a very fragmentary state, some of the deficiencies being supplied by short pieces of prose. There are two motives in the story: the Swan-maids, and the Vengeance of the Captive Smith. Three brothers, Slagfinn, Egil and Völund, sons of the Finnish King, while out hunting built themselves a house by the lake in Wolfsdale. There, early one

---

[14]Dr. Rydberg formulates a theory identifying Völund with Thiazi, the giant who carried off Idunn. It is based chiefly on arguments from names and other philological considerations, and gives perhaps undue weight to the authority of Saxo. It is difficult to see any fundamental likenesses in the stories.

The Old English references to Weland are in the *Waldere* fragment and the *Lament of Deor*. For the Franks Casket, see Professor Napier's discussion, with photographs, in the *English Miscellany* (Oxford, Clarendon Press, 1901). The *Thidreks Saga* (sometimes called *Vilkina Saga*), was edited by Unger (Christiania, 1853), and by Hylten-Cavallius (1880). There are two German translations: by Rassmann (*Heldensage*, (1863), and by Von der Hagen (*Nordische Heldenromane*, 1873).

morning, they saw three Valkyries spinning, their swancoats lying beside them. The brothers took them home; but after seven years the swan-maidens, wearied of their life, flew away to battle, and did not return.

"Seven years they stayed there, but in the eighth longing seized them, and in the ninth need parted them." Egil and Slagfinn went to seek their wives, but Völund stayed where he was and worked at his forge. There Nithud, King of Sweden, took him captive:

"Men went by night in studded mailcoats; their shields shone by the waning moon. They dismounted from the saddle at the hall-gable, and went in along the hall. They saw rings strung on bast which the hero owned, seven hundred in all; they took them off and put them on again, all but one. The keen-eyed archer Völund came in from hunting, from a far road.... He sat on a bear-skin and counted his rings, and the prince of the elves missed one; he thought Hlodve's daughter, the fairy-maid, had come back. He sat so long that he fell asleep, and awoke powerless: heavy bonds were on his hands, and fetters clasped on his feet."

They took him away and imprisoned him, ham-strung, on an island to forge treasures for his captors. Then Völund planned vengeance:

"'I see on Nithud's girdle the sword which I knew keenest and best, and which I forged with all my skill. The glittering blade is taken from me for ever; I shall not see it borne to Völund's smithy. Now Bödvild wears my bride's red ring; I expect no atonement.' He sat and slept not, but struck with his hammer."

Nithud's children came to see him in his smithy: the two boys he slew, and made drinking-cups for Nithud from their skulls; and the daughter Bödvild he beguiled, and having made himself wings he rose into the air and left her weeping for her lover and Nithud mourning his sons.

In the Old English poems allusion is made only to the second part of the story; there is no reference to the legend of the enchanted brides, which is indeed distinct in origin, being identical with the common tale of the fairy wife who is obliged to return to animal shape through some breach of agreement by her mortal husband. This incident of the compact (*i.e.*, to hide the swan-coat, to refrain from asking the wife's name, or whatever it may have been) has been lost in the Völund tale. The Continental version is told in the late Icelandic *Thidreks Saga*, where it is brought into connexion with the Volsung story; in this the story of the second brother, Egil the archer, is also given, and its antiquity is supported by the pictures on the Anglo-Saxon carved whale-bone box known as the Franks Casket, dated by Professor Napier at about 700 A.D. The adventures of the third brother, Slagfinn, have not survived. The Anglo-Saxon gives Völund and Bödvild a son, Widia or Wudga, the Wittich who appears as a follower of Dietrich's in the Continental German sources.

The Edda: The Divine & Heroic Mythology of the North

The Volsungs.—No story better illustrates the growth of heroic legend than the Volsung cycle[15]. It is composite, four or five mythical motives combining to form the nucleus; and as it took possession more and more strongly of the imagination of the early Germans, and still more of the Scandinavians, other heroic cycles were brought into dependence on it. None of the Eddic poems on the subject are quite equal in poetic value to the Helgi lays; many are fragmentary, several late, and only one attempts a review of the whole story. The outline is as follows: Sigurd the Volsung, son of Sigmund and brother of Sinfjötli, slays the dragon who guards the Nibelungs' hoard on the Glittering Heath, and thus inherits the curse which accompanies the treasure; he finds and wakens Brynhild the Valkyrie, lying in an enchanted sleep guarded by a ring of fire, loves her and plights troth with her; Grimhild, wife of the Burgundian Giuki, by enchantment causes him to forget the Valkyrie, to love her own daughter Gudrun, and, since he alone can cross the fire, to win Brynhild for her son

---

[15]As divided in most editions the poems connected with the Volsung cycle, including the two on Ermanric, are fifteen in number: *Gripisspa*; *Reginsmal, Fafnismal, Sigrdrifumal*, a continued narrative compiled from different sources; *Sigurd Fragment*, on the death of Sigurd; *First Gudrun Lay*, on Gudrun's mourning, late; *Short Sigurd Lay* (called *Long Brynhild Lay* in the *Corpus Poeticum*; sometimes called *Third Sigurd Lay*). style late; *Brynhild's Hellride*, a continuation of the preceding; *Second*, or *Old, Gudrun Lay*, is also late. It contains more kennings than are usual in Eddic poetry, and the picture of Gudrun's sojourn in Denmark and the tapestry she wrought with Thora Halfdan's daughter, together with the descriptions of her suitors, belong to a period which had a taste for colour and elaboration of detail; *Third Gudrun Lay*, or the *Ordeal of Gudrun* (after her marriage to Atli), is romantic in character. The Gothic hero Thjodrek (Dietrich) is introduced; *Oddrun's Lament*, in which Gunnar's death is caused by an intrigue with Atli's sister Oddrun, marks the disintegration of the Volsung legend; The two Atli Lays (*Atlakvida* and *Atlamal*, the latter of Greenland origin), deal with the death of Gunnar and Högni, and Gudrun's vengeance on Atli; *Gudrun's Lament* and *Hamthismal* belong to the Ermanric cycle.

Gunnar. After the marriage, Brynhild discovers the trick, and incites her husband and his brothers to kill Sigurd.

The series begins with a prose piece on the Death of Sinfjötli, which says that after Sinfjötli, son of Sigmund, Volsung's son (which should be Valsi's son, Volsung being a tribal, not a personal, name), had been poisoned by his stepmother Borghild, Sigmund married Hjördis, Eylimi's daughter, had a son Sigurd, and fell in battle against the race of Hunding. Sigmund, as in all other Norse sources, is said to be king in Frankland, which, like the Niderlant of the *Nibelungen Lied*, means the low lands on the Rhine. The scene of the story is always near that river: Sigurd was slain by the Rhine, and the treasure of the Rhine is quoted as proverbial in the Völund lay.

Gripisspa (the Prophecy of Gripi), which follows, is appropriately placed first of the Volsung poems, since it gives a summary of the whole story. Sigurd rides to see his mother's brother, Gripi, the wisest of men, to ask about his destiny, and the soothsayer prophesies his adventures and early death. This poem makes clear some original features of the legend which are obscured elsewhere, especially in the Gudrun set; Grimhild's treachery, and Sigurd's unintentional breach of faith to Brynhild. In the speeches of both Gripi and Sigurd, the poet shows clearly that Brynhild had the first right to Sigurd's faith, while the seer repeatedly protests his innocence in breaking it: "Thou shalt never be blamed though thou didst betray the royal maid.... No better man shall come on earth beneath the sun than thou, Sigurd." On the other hand, the poet gives no indication that Brynhild and the sleeping Valkyrie are the same, which is a sign of confusion. Like all poems in this form, *Gripisspa* is a late composition embodying earlier tradition.

The other poems are mostly episodical, though arranged so as to form a continued narrative. *Gripisspa* is followed by a compilation from two or more poems in different metres, generally divided into three parts in the editions: *Reginsmal* gives the early history of the treasure and the dragon, and Sigurd's battle with Hunding's sons; *Fafnismal*, the slaying of the dragon and the advice of the talking birds; *Sigrdrifumal*, the awakening of the Valkyrie. Then follows a fragment on the death of Sigurd. All the rest, except the poem generally called the *Third*, or *Short, Sigurd Lay* (which tells of the marriage with Gudrun and Sigurd's wooing of Brynhild for Gunnar) continue the story after Sigurd's death, taking up the death of Brynhild, Gudrun's mourning, and the fates of the other heroes who became connected with the legend of the treasure.

In addition to the poems in the Elder Edda, an account of the story is given by Snorri in *Skaldskaparmal*[16], but it is founded almost entirely on the surviving lays. *Völsunga Saga* is also a paraphrase, but more valuable, since parts of it are founded on lost poems, and it therefore, to some extent, represents independent tradition. It was, unfortunately from a literary point of view, compiled after the great saga-time was over, in the decadent fourteenth century, when material of all kinds, classical, biblical, romantic, mythological, was hastily cast into saga-form. It is not, like the *Nibelungen Lied*,[17] a work

---

[16]*Skaldskaparmal*, *Völsunga Saga* and *Norna-Gests Thattr* (containing another short paraphrase) are all included in Dr. Wilken's *Die Prosaische Edda* (Paderborn, 1878). There is an English version of *Völsunga* by Magnusson and Morris (London, 1870) and a German version of *Völsunga* and *Norna-Gest* by Edzardi.

[17]Editions by Bartsch (Leipzig, 1895) and Zarncke (Halle, 1899); translation into modern German by Simrock.

of art, but it has what in this case is perhaps of greater importance, the one great virtue of fidelity. The compiler did not, like the author of the German masterpiece, boldly recast his material in the spirit of his own time; he clung closely to his originals, only trying with hesitating hand to copy the favourite literary form of the Icelander. As a saga, therefore, *Völsunga* is far behind not only such great works as *Njala*, but also many of the smaller sagas. It lacks form, and is marred by inconsistencies; it is often careless in grammar and diction; it is full of traces of the decadent romantic age. Sigurd, in the true spirit of romance, is endowed with magic weapons and supernatural powers, which are no improvement on the heroic tradition, "Courage is better than a good sword." At every turn, Odin is at hand to help him, which tends to efface the older and truer picture of the hero with all the fates against him; such heroes, found again and again in the historic sagas, more truly represent the heathen heroic age and that belief in the selfishness and caprice of the Gods on which the whole idea of sacrifice rests. There is also the inevitable deterioration in the character of Brynhild, without the compensating elevation in that of her rival by which the *Nibelungen Lied* places Chriemhild on a height as lofty and unapproachable as that occupied by the Norse Valkyrie; the Brynhild of *Völsunga Saga* is something of a virago, the Gudrun is jealous and shrewish. But for actual material, the compiler is absolutely to be trusted; and *Völsunga Saga* is therefore, in spite of artistic faults, a priceless treasure-house for the real features of the legend.

There are two main elements in the Volsung story: the slaying of the dragon, and the awakening and desertion of Brynhild. The latter is brought into close connexion with the former, which becomes the real centre of the action. In the Anglo-Saxon reference, the fragment in *Beowulf*, the second episode does not appear.

In this, the oldest version of the story, which, except for a vague reference to early feats by Sigmund and Sinfjötli, consists solely of the dragon adventure, the hero is not Sigurd, but Sigemund the Waelsing. All that it tells is that Sigemund, Fitela (Sinfjötli) not being with him, killed the dragon, the guardian of the hoard, and loaded a ship with the treasure. The few preceding lines only mention the war which Sigmund and Sinfjötli waged on their foes. They are there uncle and nephew, and there is no suggestion of the closer relationship assigned to them by *Völsunga Saga*, which tells their story in full.[18]

---

[18]Saxo Grammaticus (Book vii.) tells the story of a Signy, daughter of Sigar, whose lover Hagbard, after slaying her brothers, wins her favour. Sigar in vengeance had him strangled on a hill in view of Signy's windows, and she set fire to her house that she might die simultaneously with her lover. The antiquity of part at least of this story is proved by the kenning "Hagbard's collar" for halter, in a poem probably of the tenth century. On the other hand, a reference in *Völsunga Saga*, that "Haki and Hagbard were great and famous men, yet Sigar carried off their sister, ... and they were slow to vengeance," shows that there is confusion somewhere. It seems possible that Hagbard's story has been contaminated with a distorted account of the Volsung Signy, civilised as usual by Saxo, with an effect of vulgarity absent from the primitive story.

In a recently published pamphlet by Mr. W.W. Lawrence and Dr. W.H. Schofield (*The First Riddle of Cynewulf* and *Signy's Lament*. Baltimore: The Modern Language Association of America. 1902) it is suggested that the so-called First Riddle in the Exeter Book is in reality an Anglo-Saxon translation of a Norse "Complaint" spoken by the Volsung Signy. Evidence from metre and form is all in favour of this view, and the poem bears the interpretation without any straining of the meaning. Dr. Schofield's second contention, that the poem thus interpreted is evidence for the theory of a British origin for the Eddie poems, is not equally convincing. The existence in Anglo-Saxon of a translation from the Norse is no proof that any of the Eddie poems, or even the original Norse "Signy's Lament" postulated by Dr. Schofield, were composed in the West.

It seems unnecessary to suppose, with Dr. Schofield, an influence of British legend on the

Winifred Faraday

Sigmund, one of the ten sons of Volsung (who is himself of miraculous birth) and the Wishmaiden Hlod, is one of the chosen heroes of Odin. His twin-sister Signy is married against her will to Siggeir, an hereditary enemy, and at the wedding-feast Odin enters and thrusts a sword up to the hilt into the tree growing in the middle of the hall. All try to draw it, but only the chosen Sigmund succeeds. Siggeir, on returning to his own home with his unwilling bride, invites her father and brothers to a feast. Though suspecting treachery, they come, and are killed one after another, except Sigmund who is secretly saved by his sister and hidden in the wood. She meditates revenge, and as her two sons grow up to the age of ten, she tests their courage, and finding it wanting makes Sigmund kill both: the expected hero must be a Volsung through both parents. She therefore visits Sigmund in disguise, and her third son, Sinfjötli, is the child of the Volsung pair. At ten years old, she sends him to live in the wood with Sigmund, who only knows him as Signy's son. For years they live as wer-wolves in the wood, till the time comes for vengeance. They set fire to Siggeir's hall; and Signy, after revealing Sinfjötli's real parentage, goes back into the fire and dies there, her vengeance achieved:

"I killed my children, because I thought them too weak to avenge our father; Sinfjötli has a warrior's might because he is both son's son and daughter's son to King Volsung. I have laboured to this end, that King Siggeir should meet his death; I have so toiled for the achieving

---

Volsung story. The points in which the story of Sigmund resembles that of Arthur and differs from that of Theseus prove nothing in the face of equally strong points of correspondence between Arthur and Theseus which are absent from the Volsung story.

of revenge that I am now on no condition fit for life. As I lived by force with King Siggeir, of free will shall I die with him."[19]

Though no poem survives on this subject, the story is certainly primitive; its savage character vouches for its antiquity. *Völsunga* then reproduces the substance of the prose *Death of Sinfjötli* mentioned above, the object of which, as a part of the cycle, seems to be to remove Sinfjötli and leave the field clear for Sigurd. It preserves a touch which may be original in Sinfjötli's burial, which resembles that of Scyld in *Beowulf*: his father lays him in a boat steered by an old man, which immediately disappears.

Sigmund and Sinfjötli[20] are always close comrades, "need-companions" as the Anglo-Saxon calls them. They are indivisible and form one story. Sigurd, on the other hand, is only born after his father Sigmund's death. *Völsunga* says that Sigmund fell in battle against Hunding, through the interference of Odin, who, justifying Loki's taunt that he "knew not how to give the victory fairly," shattered with his spear the sword he had given to the Volsung. For this again we have to depend entirely on the prose, except for one line in *Hyndluljod*: "The Father of Hosts gives gold to his followers;... he

---

[19]Munch (*Nordmændenes Gudelære*, Christiania, 1847) ingeniously identified the old man with Odin, come in person to conduct Sinfjötli to Valhalla, since he would otherwise have gone to Hel, not having fallen in battle; a stratagem quite in harmony with Odin's traditional character.

[20]It seems probable, on the evidence of *Beowulf*, that Sigmund and Sinfjötli represent the Pan-Germanic stage of the national-hero, and Sigurd or Siegfried the Continental stage. Possibly Helgi may then be the Norse race-hero. Sigurd was certainly foreign to Scandinavia; hence the epithet Hunnish, constantly applied to him, and the localising of the legend by the Rhine. The possibility suggests itself that the Brynhild part of the story, on the other hand, is of Scandinavian origin, and thence passed to Germany. It is at least curious that the *Nibelungen Lied* places Prunhilt in Iceland.

gave Sigmund a sword." And from the poems too, Sigurd's fatherless childhood is only to be inferred from an isolated reference, where giving himself a false name he says to Fafni: "I came a motherless child; I have no father like the sons of men." Sigmund, dying, left the fragments of the sword to be given to his unborn son, and Sigurd's fosterfather Regin forged them anew for the future dragon-slayer. But Sigurd's first deed was to avenge on Hunding's race the death of his father and his mother's father. *Völsunga* tells this story first of Helgi and Sinfjötli, then of Sigurd, to whom the poems also attribute the deed. It is followed by the dragon-slaying.

Up to this point, the story of Sigurd consists roughly of the same features which mark that of Sigmund and Sinfjötli. Both are probably, like Helgi, versions of a race-hero myth. In each case there is the usual irregular birth, in different forms, both familiar; a third type, the miraculous or supernatural birth, is attributed by *Völsunga* to Sigmund's father Volsung. Each story again includes a deed of vengeance, and a dragon and treasure. The sword which the hero alone could draw, and the wer-wolf, appear only in the Sigmund and Sinfjötli version. Among those Germanic races which brought the legend to full perfection, Sigurd's version soon became the sole one, and Sigmund and Sinfjötli practically drop out.

The Dragon legend of the Edda is much fuller and more elaborate than that of any other mythology. As a rule tradition is satisfied with the existence of the monster "old and proud of his treasure," but here we are told its full previous history, certain features of which (such as the shape-shifting) are signs of antiquity, whether it was originally connected with the Volsungs or not.

As usual, *Völsunga* gives the fullest account, in the form of a story told by Regin to his foster-son Sigurd, to incite him to slay the dragon. Regin was one of three brothers, the sons of Hreidmar; one of the three, Otr, while in the water in otter's shape, was seen by three of the Aesir, Odin, Loki and Hoeni, and killed by Loki. Hreidmar demanded as wergild enough gold to fill the otter's skin, and Loki obtained it by catching the dwarf Andvari, who lived in a waterfall in the form of a fish, and allowing him to ransom his head by giving up his wealth. One ring the dwarf tried to keep back, but in vain; and thereupon he laid a curse upon it: that the ring with the rest of the gold should be the death of whoever should get possession of it. In giving the gold to Hreidmar, Odin also tried to keep back the ring, but had to give it up to cover the last hair. Then Fafni, one of the two remaining sons, killed his father, first victim of the curse, for the sake of the gold. He carried it away and lay guarding it in the shape of a snake. But Regin the smith did not give up his hopes of possessing the hoard: he adopted as his foster-son Sigurd the Volsung, thus getting into his power the hero fated to slay the dragon.

The curse thus becomes the centre of the action, and the link between the two parts of the story, since it directly accounts for Sigurd's unconscious treachery and his separation from Brynhild, and absolves the hero from blame by making him a victim of fate. It destroys in turn Hreidmar, the Dragon, his brother Regin, the dragon-slayer himself, Brynhild (to whom he gave the ring), and the Giukings, who claimed inheritance after Sigurd's death. Later writers carried its effects still further.

This narrative is also told in the pieces of prose interspersed through *Reginsmal*. The verse consists only of scraps of dialogue. The first of these comprises question and answer between Loki and the dwarf Andvari in the form of the old riddle-poems, and seems to result from the confusion of two ideas: the question-and-answer wager, and the captive's ransom by treasure. Then follows the curse, in less general terms than in the prose: "My gold shall be the death of two brothers, and cause strife among eight kings; no one shall rejoice in the possession of my treasure." Next comes a short dialogue between Loki and Hreidmar, in which the former warns his host of the risk he runs in taking the hoard. In the next fragment Hreidmar calls on his daughters to avenge him; Lyngheid replies that they cannot do so on their own brother, and her father bids her bear a daughter whose son may avenge him. This has given rise to a suggestion that Hjördis, Sigurd's mother, was daughter to Lyngheid, but if that is intended, it may only be due to the Norse passion for genealogy. The next fragment brings Regin and Sigurd together, and the smith takes the young Volsung for his foster-son. A speech of Sigurd's follows, in which he refuses to seek the treasure till he has avenged his father on Hunding's sons. The rest of the poem is concerned with the battle with Hunding's race, and Sigurd's meeting with Odin by the way.

The fight with Fafni is not described in verse, very little of this poetry being in narrative form; but *Fafnismal* gives a dialogue between the wounded dragon and his slayer. Fafni warns the Volsung against the hoard: "The ringing gold and the glowing treasure, the rings shall be thy death." Sigurd disregards the warning with the maxim "Every man must die some time," and asks questions of the dragon in the manner of *Vafthrudnismal*. Fafni, after repeating his warning, speaks of his brother's intended treachery: "Regin betrayed me, he will betray thee; he will be the death of both of us," and dies. Regin returning bids Sigurd roast Fafni's heart, while he sleeps. A prose-piece tells that Sigurd burnt his fingers by touching the heart, put them in his mouth, and understood the speech of birds. The advice given him by the birds is taken from two different poems, and partly repeats itself; the substance is a warning to Sigurd against the treachery plotted by Regin, and a counsel to prevent it by killing him, and so become sole owner of the hoard. Sigurd takes advantage of the warning: "Fate shall not be so strong that Regin shall give my death-sentence: both brothers shall go quickly hence to Hel." Regin's enjoyment of the hoard is therefore short. The second half of the story begins when one of the birds, after a reference to Gudrun, guides Sigurd to the sleeping Valkyrie:

"Bind up the red rings, Sigurd; it is not kingly to fear. I know a maid, fairest of all, decked with gold, if thou couldst get her. Green roads lead to Giuki's, fate guides the wanderer forward. There a mighty king has a daughter; Sigurd will buy her with a dowry. There is a hall high on Hindarfell; all without it is swept with fire.... I know a battle-maid who sleeps on the fell, and the flame plays over her; Odin touched the maid with a thorn, because she laid low others than those he wished to fall. Thou shalt see, boy, the helmed maid who rode Vingskorni from the fight; Sigrdrifa's sleep cannot be broken, son of heroes, by the Norns' decrees."

Sigrdrifa (dispenser of victory) is, of course, Brynhild; the name may have been originally an epithet of the Valkyrie, and it was probably such passages as this that misled the author of *Gripisspa* into differentiating the Valkyrie and Brynhild. The last lines have been differently interpreted as a warning to Sigurd not to seek Brynhild and an attempt to incite him to do so by emphasising the difficulty of the deed; they may merely mean that her sleep cannot be broken except by one, namely, the one who knows no fear. Brynhild's supernatural origin is clearly shown here, and also in the prose in *Sigrdrifumal*. *Völsunga Saga*, though it paraphrases in full the passages relating to the magic sleep, removes much of the mystery surrounding her by providing her with a genealogy and family connections; while the *Nibelungen Lied* goes further still in the same direction by leaving out the magic sleep. The change is a natural result of Christian ideas, to which Odin's Wishmaidens would become incomprehensible.

Thus far the story is that of the release of the enchanted princess, popularly most familiar in the nursery tale of the Sleeping Beauty. After her broken questions to her deliverer, "What cut my mail? How have I broken from sleep? Who has flung from me the dark spells?" and his answer, "Sigmund's son and Sigurd's sword," she bursts into the famous "Greeting to the World":

"Long have I slept, long was I sunk in sleep, long are men's misfortunes. It was Odin's doing that I could not break the runes of sleep. Hail, day! hail, sons of day! hail, night! Look on us two with gracious eyes, and give victory to us who sit here. Hail, Aesir! hail, Asynjor! hail, Earth, mother of all! give eloquence and wisdom to us the wonderful pair, and hands of healing while we live."

She then becomes Sigurd's guardian and protectress and the

source of his wisdom, as she speaks the runes and counsels which are to help him in all difficulties; and from this point corresponds to the maiden who is the hero's benefactress, but whom he deserts through sorcery: the "Mastermaid" of the fairy-tales, the Medeia of Greek myth. Gudrun is always an innocent instrument in drawing Sigurd away from his real bride, the actual agent being her witch-mother Grimhild. This part of the story is summarised in *Gripisspa*, except that the writer seems unaware that the Wishmaiden who teaches Sigurd "every mystery that men would know" and the princess he betrays are the same:

"A king's daughter bright in mail sleeps on the fell; thou shalt hew with thy sharp sword, and cut the mail with Fafni's slayer.... She will teach thee every mystery that men would know, and to speak in every man's tongue.... Thou shalt visit Heimi's dwelling and be the great king's joyous guest.... There is a maid fair to see at Heimi's; men call her Brynhild, Budli's daughter, but the great king Heimi fosters the proud maid.... Heimi's fair foster-daughter will rob thee of all joy; thou shalt sleep no sleep, and judge no cause, and care for no man unless thou see the maiden. ... Ye shall swear all binding oaths but keep few when thou hast been one night Giuki's guest, thou shalt not remember Heimi's brave foster-daughter.... Thou shalt suffer treachery from another and pay the price of Grimhild's plots. The bright-haired lady will offer thee her daughter."

Völsunga gives additional details: Brynhild knows her deliverer to be Sigurd Sigmundsson and the slayer of Fafni, and they swear oaths to each other. The description of their second meeting, when he finds her among her maidens, and she prophesies that he will marry

Giuki's daughter, and also the meeting between her and Gudrun before the latter's marriage, represent a later development of the story, inconsistent with the older conception of the Shield-maiden. Sigurd gives Brynhild the ring Andvaranaut, which belonged to the hoard, as a pledge, and takes it from her again later when he woos her in Gunnar's form. It is the sight of the ring afterwards on Gudrun's hand which reveals to her the deception; but the episode has also a deeper significance, since it brings her into connection with the central action by passing the curse on to her. According to Snorri's paraphrase, Sigurd gives the ring to Brynhild when he goes to her in Gunnar's form.

For the rest of the story we must depend chiefly on *Gripisspa* and *Völsunga*. The latter tells that Grimhild, the mother of the Giukings, gave Sigurd a magic drink by which he forgot Brynhild and fell in love with Giuki's daughter. Gudrun's brothers swore oaths of friendship with him, and he agreed to ride through the waverlowe, or ring of fire, disguised and win Brynhild for the eldest brother Gunnar. After the two bridals, he remembered his first passing through the flame, and his love for Brynhild returned. The Shield-maiden too remembered, but thinking that Gunnar had fairly won her, accepted her fate until Gudrun in spite and jealousy revealed the trick that had been played on her. Of the treachery of the Giukings Brynhild takes little heed; but death alone can pay for Sigurd's unconscious betrayal. She tells Gunnar that Sigurd has broken faith with him, and the Giukings with some reluctance murder their sister's husband. Brynhild springs on to the funeral pyre, and dies with Sigurd. *Völsunga* makes the murder take place in Sigurd's chamber, and one poem, the *Short Sigurd Lay*, agrees. The fragment which follows *Sigrdrifumal*, on the other hand, places the scene in the open air:

"Sigurd was slain south of the Rhine; a raven on a tree called aloud: 'On you will Atli redden the sword; your broken oaths shall destroy you.' Gudrun Giuki's daughter stood without, and these were the first words she spoke: 'Where is now Sigurd, the lord of men, that my kinsmen ride first?' Högni alone made answer: 'We have hewn Sigurd asunder with the sword; the grey horse still stoops over his dead lord.'"

This agrees with the *Old Gudrun Lay* and with the Continental German version, as a prose epilogue points out.

Of the Giuking brothers, Gunnar appears only in a contemptible light: he gains his bride by treachery, and keeps his oath to Sigurd by a quibble. Högni, who has little but his name in common with Hagen von Tronje of the *Nibelungen Lied*, advises Gunnar against breaking his oath, but it is he who taunts Gudrun afterwards. The later poems of the cycle try to make heroes out of both; the same discrepancy exists between the first and second halves of the *Nibelungen Lied*. Their half-brother, Gutthorm, plays no part in the story except as the actual murderer of Sigurd.

The chief effect of the influences of Christianity and Romance on the legend is a loss of sympathy with the heroic type of Brynhild, and an attempt to give more dignity to the figure of Gudrun. The Shield-maiden of divine origin and unearthly wisdom, with her unrelenting vengeance on her beloved, and her contempt for her slighter rival ("Fitter would it be for Gudrun to die with Sigurd, if she had a soul like mine"), is a figure out of harmony with the new religion, and beyond the comprehension of a time coloured by romance; while both the sentiment and the morality of the age would be on the side of Gudrun as the formally wedded wife. So the poem known as the *Short Sigurd Lay*, which has many marks of lateness, such as the elaborate description of the funeral pyre and the exaggeration of the signs of mourning, says nothing of Sigurd's love for Brynhild, nor do his last words to Gudrun give any hint of it. The *Nibelungen Lied* suppresses Sigurd's love to Brynhild, and the magic drink, and altogether lowers Brynhild, but elevates Gudrun (under her mother's name); her slow but terrible vengeance, and absolute forgetfulness of the ties of blood in pursuit of it, are equal to anything in the original version. The later heroic poems of the Edda make a less successful attempt to create sympathy for Gudrun; some, such as the so-called *First Gudrun Lay*, which is entirely romantic in character, try to make her pathetic by the abundance of tears she sheds; others, to make her heroic, though the result is only a spurious savagery.

The remaining poems of the cycle, all late in style and tone, deal with the fates of Gudrun and her brothers, and owe their existence to a narrator's unwillingness to let a favourite story end. The curse makes continuation easy, since the Giukings inherit it with the hoard. Gudrun was married at the wish of her kinsmen to Atli the Hun, said to be Brynhild's brother. He invited Gunnar and Högni to his court and killed them for the sake of the treasure, in vengeance for which Gudrun killed her own two sons and Atli; this latter incident being possibly an imitation of Signy. If we may believe that Gudrun, like

Chriemhild in the *Nibelungen Lied*[21], married Atli in order to gain vengeance for Sigurd, we might suppose that there was confusion here: that she herself incited the murder of her brothers, and killed Atli when he had served his purpose. This would strengthen the part of Gudrun, who as the tale stands is rather a futile character. But in all probability the episode is due to a confusion of Signy's story with that of the German Chriemhild and Etzel.

One point has still to be considered: the place of the Nibelungs in the story. In the Edda, the Hniflungs are always the Giukings, Gunnar and Högni, and Snorri gives it as the name of an heroic family. The title of the first *aventiure* of the *Nibelungen Lied* also apparently uses the word of the Burgundians. Yet the treasure is always the Nibelungs' hoard, which clearly means that they were the original owners; and when Hagen von Tronje tells the story later in the poem, he speaks of the Nibelungs correctly as the dwarfs from whom Siegfried won it. On this point, therefore, the German preserves the older tradition: the Norse Andvari, the river-dwarf, is the German Alberich the Nibelung. In the *Nibelungen Lied* the winning of the treasure forms no part of the action: it is merely narrated by Hagen. This accounts for the shortening of the episode

---

[21] Wagner's *Ring des Nibelungen* is remarkable not only for the way in which it reproduces the spirit of both the Sinfjötli and the Sigurd traditions, but also for the wonderful instinct which chooses the best and most Page 56primitive features of both Norse and Continental versions. Thus he keeps the dragon of the Norse, the Nibelungs of the German; preserves the wildness of the old Sigmund tale, and substitutes the German Hagen for his paler Norse namesake; restores the original balance between the parts of Brynhild and Gudrun; gives the latter character, and an active instead of a passive function in the story, by assigning to her her mother's share in the action; and by substituting for the slaying of the otter the bargain with the Giants for the building of Valhalla, makes the cause worthy of the catastrophe.

and the omission of the intermediate steps: the robbing of the dwarf, the curse, and the dragon-slaying.

* * * * *

Ermanric.—The two poems of *Gudrun's Lament* and *Hamthismal*, in the Edda attached to the Volsung cycle, belong correctly to that of the Gothic hero Ermanric[22]. According to these poems, Gudrun, Giuki's daughter, married a third time, and had three sons, Sörli, Hamthi and Erp. She married Svanhild, her own and Sigurd's daughter, to Jörmunrek, king of the Goths; but Svanhild was slandered, and her husband had her trodden to death by horses' hoofs. The description of Svanhild is a good example of the style of the romantic poems:

"The bondmaids sat round Svanhild, dearest of my children; Svanhild was like a glorious sunbeam in my hall. I dowered her with gold and goodly fabrics when I married her into Gothland. That was the hardest of my griefs, when they trod Svanhild's fair hair into the dust beneath the horses' hoofs."

Gudrun sent her three sons to avenge their sister; two of them slew Erp by the way, and were killed themselves in their attack on Jörmunrek for want of his help. So died, as Snorri says, all who were of Giuking descent; and only Aslaug, daughter of Sigurd and Brynhild, survived. *Heimskringla*, a thirteenth century history of the royal races of Scandinavia, traces the descent of the Norse kings from her.

---

[22]For examples of legend becoming attached to historical names, see Tylor's *Primitive Culture*.

This Ermanric story, which belongs to legendary history rather than myth, is in reality quite independent of the Volsung or Nibelung cycle. The connection is loose and inartistic, the legend being probably linked to Gudrun's name because she had become a favourite character and Icelandic narrators were unwilling to let her die. The historic Ermanric was conquered by the Huns in 374; the sixth century historian Jornandes is the earliest authority for the tradition that he was murdered by Sarus and Ammius in revenge for their sister's death by wild horses. Saxo also tells the story, with greater similarity of names. It seems hardly necessary to assume, with many scholars, the existence of two heroes of the name Ermanric, an historic and a mythical one. A simpler explanation is that a legendary story became connected with the name of a real personage. The slaying of Erp introduces a common folk-tale incident, familiar in stories like the *Golden Bird*, told by both Asbjörnsen and Grimm.

* * * * *

Helgi.—The Helgi-lays[23], three in number, are the best of the heroic poems. Nominally they tell two stories, Helgi Hjörvardsson being sandwiched between the two poems of Helgi Hundingsbane; but essentially the stories are the same.

In *Helyi Hjörvardsson*, Helgi, son of Hjörvard and Sigrlinn, was dumb and nameless until a certain day when, while sitting on a howe, he saw a troop of nine Valkyries. The fairest, Svava, Eylimi's daughter,

---

[23]The Helgi Lays stand before the Volsung set in the MS.; I treat them later for the sake of greater clearness.

named him, and bidding him avenge his grandfather on Hrodmar (a former wooer of Sigrlinn's, and her father's slayer), sent him to find a magic sword. Helgi slew Hrodmar and married Svava, having escaped from the sea-giantess Hrimgerd through the protection of his Valkyrie bride and the wit of a faithful servant. His brother Hedin, through the spells of a troll-wife, swore to wed Helgi's bride. Repenting, he told his brother, who, dying in a fight with Hrodmar's son, charged Svava to marry Hedin. A note by the collector adds "Helgi and Svava are said to have been born again."

In *Helgi Hundingsbane I.*, Helgi is the son of Sigmund and Borghild. He fought and slew Hunding, and afterwards met in battle Hunding's sons at Logafell, where the Valkyrie Sigrun, Högni's daughter, protected him, and challenged him to fight Hödbrodd to whom her father had plighted her. She protected his ships in the storm which overtook them as they sailed to meet Hödbrodd, and watched over him in the battle, in which he slew his rival and was greeted as victor by Sigrun: "Hail, hero of Yngvi's race ... thou shalt have both the red rings and the mighty maid: thine are Högni's daughter and Hringstad, the victory and the land."

Helgi Hundingsbane II., besides giving additional details of the hero's early life, completes the story. In the battle with Hödbrodd, Helgi killed all Sigrun's kinsmen except one brother, Dag, who slew him later in vengeance. But Helgi returned from the grave, awakened by Sigrun's weeping, and she went into the howe with him. The collector again adds a note: "Helgi and Sigrun are said to have been born again: he was then called Helgi Haddingjaskati, and she Kara Halfdan's daughter, as it is told in the Kara-ljod, and she was a Valkyrie." [24]

---

[24]*Hromundar Saga Gripssonar*, in which this story is given, is worthless as literature, and has

This third Helgi legend does not survive in verse, the *Kara-ljod* having perished. It is told in prose in the late saga of Hromund Gripsson, according to which Kara was a Valkyrie and swan-maid: while she was hovering over Helgi, he killed her accidentally in swinging his sword.

There can be little doubt that these three are merely variants of the same story; the foundation is the same, though incidents and names differ. The three Helgis are one hero, and the three versions of his legend probably come from different localities. The collector could not but feel their identity, and the similarity was too fundamental to be overlooked; he therefore accounted for it by the old idea of re-birth, and thus linked the three together. In each Helgi has an hereditary foe (Hrodmar, Hunding, or Hadding); in each his bride is a Valkyrie, who protects him and gives him victory; each ends in tragedy, though differently.[25]

The two variants in the Poetic Edda have evident marks of contamination with the Volsung cycle, and some points of superficial resemblance. Helgi Hjörvardsson's mother is Sigrlinn, Helgi

---

not been recently edited. P.E. Müller's *Sagabibliothek*, in which it was published, is out of print. Latin and Swedish translations may be found in Björner's *Nordiske Kåmpa Dater* (Stockholm, 1737), also out of print.

[25]Dr. Storm has an interesting article on the Norse belief in Re-birth in the *Arkiv for Nordisk Filologi*, ix. He collects instances, and among other arguments points out the Norse custom of naming a posthumous child after its dead father as a probable relic of the belief. The inheritance of luck may perhaps be another survival; a notable instance occurs in *Viga-Glums Saga*, where the warrior Vigfus bequeaths his luck to his favourite grandson, Glum. In the *Waterdale Saga* there are two instances in which it is stated that the luck of the dead grandfather will pass to the grandson who receives his name. Scholars do not, however, agree as to the place of the rebirth idea in the Helgi poems, some holding the view that it is an essential part of the story.

Hundings-bane's father is Sigmund, as in the *Nibelungen Lied* Siegfried is the son of Sigemunt and Sigelint. Helgi Hundingsbane is a Volsung and Wolfing (Ylfing), and brother to Sinfjötli; his first fight, like Sigurd's, is against the race of Hunding; his rival, Hödbrodd, is a Hniflung; he first meets the Valkyrie on Loga-fell (Flame-hill); he is killed by his brother-in-law, who has sworn friendship. But there is no parallel to the essential features of the Volsung cycle, and such likenesses between the two stories as are not accidental are due to the influence of the more favoured legend; this is especially true of the names. The prose-piece *Sinfjötli's Death* also makes Helgi half-brother to Sinfjötli; it is followed in this by *Völsunga Saga*, which devotes a chapter to Helgi, paraphrasing *Helyi Hundingsbane I*. There is, of course, confusion over the Hunding episode; the saga is obliged to reconcile its conflicting authorities by making Helgi kill Hunding and some of his sons, and Sigurd kill the rest.

If the theory stated below as to the original Helgi legend be correct, the feud with Hunding's race, as told in these poems, must be extraneous. I conjecture that it belonged originally to the Volsung cycle, and to the werwolf Sinfjötli[26]. It must not be forgotten that, though he passes out of the Volsung story altogether in the later versions, both Scandinavian and German, he is in the main action in the earliest one (that in *Beowulf*), where even Sigurd does not appear.

---

[26]It is possible that the werwolf story is a totem survival. If so, the Hunding feud might easily belong to it: dogs are the natural enemies of wolves. It is curious that the Irish werwolf Cormac has a feud with MacCon (*i.e.*, Son of a Dog), which means the same as Hunding. This story, which has not been printed, will be found in the Bodleian MS. Laud, 610.

The feud might easily have been transferred from him to Helgi as well as to Sigurd, for invention is limited as regards episodes, and a narrator who wishes to elaborate the story of a favourite hero is often forced to borrow adventures. In the original story, Helgi's blood-feud was probably with the kindred of Sigrun or Svava.

The origin of the Helgi legend must be sought outside of the Volsung cycle. Some writers are of opinion that the name should be Holgi, and there are two stories in which a hero Holgi appears. With the legend of Thorgerd Holgabrud[27], told by Saxo, who identified it with that of Helgi Hundingsbane, it has nothing in common; and the connection which has been sought with the legend of Holger Danske[28] is equally difficult to establish. The essence of this latter story is the hero's disappearance into fairyland, and the expectation of his return sometime in the future: a motive which has been very fruitful in Irish romance, and in the traditions of Arthur, Tryggvason, and Barbarossa, among countless others. But it is absent from the Helgi poems; and the "old wives' tales" of Helgi's re-birth have nothing to do with his legend, but are merely a bookman's attempt to connect stories which he felt to be the same though different.

The essential feature of the story told in these poems is the motive familiar in that class of ballads of which the *Douglas Tragedy* is a type: the hero loves the daughter of his enemy's house, her kinsmen kill him, and she dies of grief. This is the story told in both the lays of

---

[27]Told in Saxo, Book ii. Snorri has a bare allusion to it.
[28]See *Corpus Poeticum Boreale*, vol. i. p. cxxx., and No. 10 of this series. The Norse version of the story (Helgi Thorisson) is told in the Saga of Olaf Tryggvason, and is summarised by Dr. Rydberg in the *Teutonic Mythology*, and by Mr. Nutt in the *Voyage of Bran*.

Helgi Hundingsbane, complete in one, unfinished in the other. No single poem preserves all the incidents of the legend; some survive in one version, some in another, as usual in ballad literature.

Like Sinfjötli and Sigurd, Helgi is brought up in obscurity. He spends his childhood disguised in his enemy's household, and on leaving it, sends a message to tell his foes whom they have fostered. They pursue him, and he is obliged, like Gude Wallace in the Scottish ballad, to disguise himself in a bondmaid's dress:

"Piercing are the eyes of Hagal's bondmaid; it is no peasant's kin who stands at the mill: the stones are split, the bin springs in two. It is a hard fate for a warrior to grind the barley; the sword-hilt is better fitted for those hands than the mill-handle."

Sigrun is present at the battle, in which, as in the English and Scottish ballads, Helgi slays all her kindred except one brother. He tells her the fortunes of the fight, and she chooses between lover and kinsmen:

Helgi. "Good luck is not granted thee, maid, in all things, though the Norns are partly to blame. Bragi and Högni fell to-day at Frekastein, and I was their slayer;... most of thy kindred lie low. Thou couldst not hinder the battle: it was thy fate to be a cause of strife to heroes. Weep not, Sigrun, thou hast been Hild to us; heroes must meet their fate."

Sigrun. "I could wish those alive who are fallen, and yet rest in thy arms."

The surviving brother, Dag, swears oaths of reconciliation to Helgi, but remembers the feud. The end comes, as in the Norse Sigmund tale, through Odin's interference: he lends his spear to Dag, who stabs Helgi in a grove, and rides home to tell his sister. Sigrun is inconsolable, and curses the murderer with a rare power and directness:

"May the oaths pierce thee that thou hast sworn to Helgi.... May the ship sail not that sails under thee, though a fair wind lie behind. May the horse run not that runs under thee, though thou art fleeing from thy foes. May the sword bite not that thou drawest, unless it sing round thine own head. If thou wert an outlaw in the woods, Helgi's death were avenged.... Never again while I live, by night or day, shall I sit happy at Sevafell, if I see not the light play on my hero's company, nor the gold-bitted War-breeze run thither with the warrior."

But Helgi returns from the grave, unable to rest because of Sigrun's weeping, and she goes down into the howe with him:

Sigrun. "Thy hair is covered with frost, Helgi; thou art drenched with deadly dew, thy hands are cold and wet. How shall I get thee help, my hero?"

Helgi. "Thou alone hast caused it, Sigrun from Sevafell, that Helgi is drenched with deadly dew. Thou weepest bitter tears before thou goest to sleep, gold-decked, sunbright, Southern maid; each one falls on my breast, bloody, cold and wet, cruel, heavy with grief...."

Sigrun. "I have made thee here a painless bed, Helgi, son of the Wolfings. I will sleep in thy arms, my warrior, as if thou wert alive."

Helgi. "There shall be no stranger thing at Sevafell, early or late, than that thou, king-born, Högni's fair daughter, shouldst be alive in the grave and sleep in a dead man's arms."

The lay of Helgi Hjörvardsson is furthest from the original, for there is no feud with Svava's kindred, nor does Helgi die at their hands; but it preserves a feature omitted elsewhere, in his leaving his bride to his brother's protection. Like the wife in the English ballad of *Earl Brand*, and the heroine of the Danish *Ribold and Guldborg*, Svava refuses, but Hedin's last words seem to imply that he is to return and marry her after avenging Helgi. This would be contrary to all parallels, according to which Svava should die with Helgi.[29]

The alternative ending of the *Helgi and Kara* version is interesting as providing the possible source of another Scottish ballad dealing with the same type of story. In *The Cruel Knight*, as here, the hero slays his bride, who is of a hostile family, by mistake. One passage of *Helgi Hundingsbane II.* describes Helgi's entrance into Valhalla, which, taken with the incident of Sigrun's joining him in the howe, supplies an instance of the survival side by side of inconsistent notions as to the state of the dead. The lover's return from the grave is the subject of *Clerk Saunders* (the second part) and several other Scottish ballads.

---

[29]Professor Child is perhaps hasty in regarding the two parts of *Clerk Saunders* as independent. The first part, though unlike the Helgi story in circumstance, seems to preserve the tradition of the hero's hostility to his bride's kindred, and his death at their hands.

The Helgi story, in all its variants, is as familiar in Danish as in Border ballads. The distribution of the material in Iceland, Denmark, England and Scotland is strongly in favour of the presumption that Scandinavian legend influenced England and Scotland, and against the presumption that the poems in question passed from the British Isles to Iceland. The evidence of the Danish ballads should be conclusive on this point. There is an English translation of the latter by R.C.A. Prior (*Ancient Danish Ballads*, London, 1860).

The Song of the Mill.—The magic mill is best known in the folk-tale, "Why the sea is salt"; but this is not the oldest part of the story, though it took most hold of the popular imagination which loves legendary explanations of natural phenomena. The hero, Frodi, a mythical Danish king, is the northern Croesus. His reign was marked by a world-peace, and the peace, the wealth, the liberality of Frodi became proverbial. The motive of his tale is again the curse that follows gold. It is told by Snorri, in whose work *Grottasöngr* is embodied.

Frodi possessed two magic quern-stones, from which the grinder could grind out whatever he wished; but he had no one strong enough to turn them until he bought in Sweden two bondmaids of giant-race, Menja and Fenja. He set them to grind at the quern by day, and by night when all slept, and as they ground him gold, and peace, and prosperity, they sang:

"We grind wealth for Frodi, all bliss we grind, and abundance of riches in the fortunate bin. May he sit on wealth, may he sleep on down, may he wake to delight; then the grinding were good. Here shall no man hurt another, prepare evil nor work death, nor hew with the keen sword though he find his brother's slayer bound."

But when they wearied of their toil and asked for a little rest, Frodi answered: "Ye shall sleep no longer than the cuckoo is silent, or while I speak one stave." Then the giant-maids grew angry, and sang:

"Thou wert not wise, Frodi, in buying thy bondmaids: thou didst choose us for our strength and size but asked not our race. Bold were Hrungni and his father, and mightier Thiazi; Idi and Orni were our ancestors, from them are we daughters of the mountain-giants sprung.... We maids wrought mighty deeds, we moved the mountains from their places, we rolled rocks over the court of the giants, so that the earth shook.... Now we are come to the king's house, meeting no mercy and held in bondage, mud beneath our feet and cold over our heads, we grind the Peace-maker. It is dreary at Frodi's."

As they sang of their wrongs by night, their mood changed, and instead of grinding peace and wealth, they ground war, fire and sword:

"Waken, Frodi! waken, Frodi! if thou wilt hear our songs.... I see fire burn at the east of the citadel, the voice of war awakes, the signal is given. A host will come hither in speed, and burn the hall over the king."

So the bondmaids ground on in giant-wrath, while the sea-king Mysing sailed nearer with his host, until the quern-stones split; and then the daughters of the mountain-giants spoke once more: "We have ground to our pleasure, Frodi; we maids have stood long at the mill."

A Norseman was rarely content to allow a fortunate ending to any hero, and a continuation of the story therefore makes the mill bring disaster on Mysing also. After slaying Frodi and burning his hall, he took the stones and the bondmaids on board his ship, and bade them grind salt. They ground till the weight sank the ship to the bottom of the sea, where the mill is grinding still. This is not in the song, though it has lived longer popularly than the earlier part. Dr. Rydberg identifies Frodi with Frey, the God of fertility.

The Everlasting Battle.—No Eddic poem survives on the battle of the Hjathnings[30], the story of which is told in prose by Snorri. It must, however, be an ancient legend; and the hero Hedin belongs to one of the old Germanic heroic races, for the minstrel Deor is a dependent of the Heodenings in the Old English poem to which reference will be made later. The legend is that Hild, daughter of Högni, was carried away by Hedin the Hjathning, Hjarrandi's son. Högni pursued, and overtook them near the Orkneys. Then Hild went to her father and offered atonement from Hedin, but said also that he was quite ready to fight, and Högni need expect no mercy. Högni answered shortly, and Hild returning told Hedin that her father would accept no atonement but bade him prepare to fight. Both kings landed on an island, followed by their men. Hedin called to Högni and offered atonement and much gold, but Högni said it was too late, his sword was already drawn. They fought till evening, and then returned to their ships; but Hild went on shore and woke up all the slain by sorcery, so that the battle began again next day just as before. Every day they fight, and every night the dead are recalled to life, and so it will go on till Ragnarök.

In the German poem, *Gudrun*, the Continental version of this

---

[30]The Skald Bragi (before 850 A.D.) has a poem on this subject, given with a translation in the *Corpus*, vol. ii. Saxo's version is in the fifth book of his History. According to Bragi, Hild has a necklace, which has caused comparison of this story with that of the Greek Eriphyle. Irish legendary history describes a similar battle in which the slain revive each night and renew the fight daily, as occurring in the wanderings of the Tuatha De Danann before they reached Ireland. According to Keating, they learnt the art of necromancy in the East, and taught it to the Danes.

The latest edition of the *Gudrun* is by Ernst Martin (second edition, Halle, 1902). There is a modern German translation by Simrock.

legend occurs in the story of the second Hilde. She is carried away by the minstrel Horant (who thus plays a more active part than the Norse Hjarrandi), as envoy from King Hettel, Hedin's German counterpart. Her father Hagen pursues, and after a battle with Hettel agrees to a reconciliation. The story is duplicated in the abduction of Hilde's daughter Gudrun, and the battle on the Wülpensand.

Another reference may probably be supplied by the much debated lines 14–16 from the Anglo-Saxon *Deor*, of which the most satisfactory translation seems to be: "Many of us have heard of the harm of Hild; the Jute's loves were unbounded, so that the care of love took from him sleep altogether." Saxo, it is true, makes Hild's father a Jute, instead of her lover, and Snorri apparently agrees with him in making Hedin Norwegian; but in the *Gudrun* Hettel is Frisian or Jutish. The Anglo-Saxon *Widsith* mentions in one line Hagena, king of the Holmrygas (a Norwegian province), and Heoden, king of the Glommas (not identified), who may be the Högni and Hedin of this tale.

The Anglo-Saxon and German agree on another point where both differ from the Norse. The Anglo-Saxon poem *Deor* is supposed to be spoken by a *scop* or court poet who has been ousted from the favour of his lord, a Heodening, by Heorrenda, another singer: "Once I was the Heodenings' scop, dear to my lord: Deor was my name. Many a year I had a good service and a gracious lord, until the song-skilled Hoerrenda received the rights which the protector of men once granted me." Like Heorrenda, Horant in the *Gudrun* is a singer in the service of the Heathnings. The Norse version keeps the name, and its connection with the Heathnings, but gives Hjarrandi, as the hero's father, no active part to play. In both points, arguing from the probable Frisian origin of the story, the Anglo-Saxon and German are more likely to have the correct form.

The legend is, like those of Walter and Hildigund, Helgi and Sigrun, founded on the primary instincts of love and war. In the Norse story of the Heathnings, however, the former element is almost eliminated. It is from no love to Hedin that Hild accompanies him, though Saxo would have it so. Nothing is clearer than that strife is her only object. It is her mediation which brings about the battle, when apparently both heroes would be quite willing to make peace; and her arts which cause the daily renewal of fighting. This island battle among dead and living is peculiar to the Norse version, and coloured by, if not originating in, the Valhalla idea: Högni and Hedin and their men are the Einherjar who fight every day and rest and feast at night, Hild is a war-goddess. The conception of her character, contrasting with the gentler part played by the Continental German heroines (who are rather the causes than the inciters of strife), can be paralleled from many of the sagas proper.[31]

Högni's sword Dainsleif, forged by the dwarfs, as were all magic weapons, is like the sword of Angantyr, in that it claims a victim whenever it is drawn from the sheath: an idea which may easily have arisen from the prowess of any famous swordsman.

---

[31]The poems of this cycle are four in number—(1) *Hjalmar's Death-song*: (2) *Angantyr and Hervör*; (3) *Heidrek's Riddle-Poem*: (4) *Angantyr the Younger and Hlod*. All are given in the first volume of the *Corpus*, with translations.
Herrarar Saga was published by Rafn (Copenhagen, 1829–30) in *Fornaldar Sögur*, vol. i., now out of print. It has been more recently edited by Dr. Bugge, together with *Völsunga* and others. Petersen (Copenhagen, 1847) edited it with a Danish translation. Munch's *Nordmuendenes Gudelære* (out of print) contains a short abstract.

The Sword of Angantyr.—Like the two last legends, Angantyr's story is not represented in the Elder Edda; it is not even told by Snorri. Yet poems belonging to the cycle survive (preserved by good fortune in the late mythical *Hervarar Saga*) which among the heroic poems rank next in artistic beauty to the Helgi Lays. Since the story possesses besides a striking originality, and is connected with the name of a Pan-Germanic hero, the Ongendtheow of Old English poetry, I cannot follow the example of most editors and omit it from the heroic poems.

Like the Volsung legend it is the story of a curse; and there is a general similarity of outline, with the exception that the hero is in this case a woman. The curse-laden treasure is here the sword Tyrfing, which Svafrlami got by force from the dwarfs. They laid a curse on it: that it should bring death to its bearer, no wound it made should be healed, and it should claim a victim whenever it was unsheathed. In the saga, the story is spread over several generations: partly, no doubt, in order to include varying versions; partly also in imitation of the true Icelandic family saga. The chief actors in the legend, beside the sword, are Angantyr[32] and his daughter Hervör.

The earlier history of Tyrfing is told in the saga. Svafrlami is killed, with the magic weapon itself, by the viking Arngrim, who thus gains possession of it; when he is slain in his turn, it descends to Angantyr, the eldest of his twelve berserk sons. For a while no one can withstand them, but the doom overtakes them at last in the battle of Samsey against the Swedes Arrow-Odd and Hjalmar. In berserk-rage,

---

[32]Angantyr's death is related by Saxo, Book v., with entire exclusion of all mythical interest.

the twelve brothers attack the Swedish ships, and slay every man except the two leaders who have landed on the island. The battle over, the berserks go ashore, and there when their fury is past, they are attacked by the two Swedish champions. Odd fights eleven of the brothers, but Hjalmar has the harder task in meeting Angantyr and his sword. All the twelve sons of Arngrim fall, and Hjalmar is mortally wounded by Tyrfing. The survivor buries his twelve foemen where they fell, and takes his comrade's body back to Sweden. The first poem gives the challenge of the Swedish champions, and Hjalmar's dying song.

Hervör, the daughter of Angantyr, is in some respects a female counterpart of Sigurd. Like him, she is born after her father's death, and brought up in obscurity. When she learns her father's name, she goes forth without delay to claim her inheritance from the dead, even with the curse that goes with it. Here the second poem begins. On reaching the island where her father fell, she asks a shepherd to guide her to the graves of Arngrim's sons:

"I will ask no hospitality, for I know not the islanders; tell me quickly, where are the graves called Hjörvard's howes?"

He is unwilling: "The man is foolish who comes here alone in the dark shade of night: fire is flickering, howes are opening, field and fen are aflame," and flees into the woods, but Hervör is dauntless and goes on alone. She reaches the howes, and calls on the sons of Arngrim:

"Awake, Angantyr! Hervör calls thee, only daughter to thee and Tofa. Give me from the howe the keen sword which the dwarfs forged for Svafrlami, Hervard, Hjörvard, Hrani, Angantyr! I call you all from below the tree-roots, with helm and corselet, with sharp sword, shield and harness, and reddened spear."

Angantyr denies that the sword is in his howe: "Neither father, son, nor other kinsmen buried me; my slayers had Tyrfing;" but Hervör does not believe him. "Tell me but truth.... Thou art slow to give thine only child her heritage." He tries to frighten her back to the ships by describing the sights she will see, but she only cries again, "Give me Hjalmar's slayer from the howe, Angantyr!"

A. "Hjalmar's slayer lies under my shoulders; it is all wrapped in fire; I know no maid on earth who dare take that sword in her hands."

H. "I will take the sharp sword in my hands, if I can get it: I fear no burning fire, the flame sinks as I look on it."

A. "Foolish art thou, Hervör the fearless, to rush into the fire open-eyed. I will rather give thee the sword from the howe, young maid; I cannot refuse thee."

H. "Thou dost well, son of vikings, to give me the sword from the howe. I think its possession better than to win all Norway."

Her father warns her of the curse, and the doom that the sword will bring, and she leaves the howes followed by his vain wish: "Would that I could give thee the lives of us twelve, the strength and energy that we sons of Arngrim left behind us!"

It is unnecessary here to continue the story as the saga does, working out the doom over later generations; over Hervör's son Heidrek, who forfeited his head to Odin in a riddle-contest, and over his children, another Angantyr, Hlod, and a second Hervör. The verse sources for this latter part are very corrupt.

A full discussion of the relation between the Eddic and the

The Edda: The Divine & Heroic Mythology of the North

Continental versions of the heroic tales summarised in the foregoing pages would, of course, be far beyond the scope of this study; the utmost that can be done in that direction is to suggest a few points. Three of the stories are not concerned in this section: Helgi and Frodi are purely Scandinavian cycles; while though Angantyr is a well-known heroic name (in *Widsith* Ongendtheow is king of the Swedes), the legend attached to his name in the Norse sources does not survive elsewhere. The Weland cycle is perhaps common property. None of the versions localise it, for the names in *Völundarkvida*, Wolfdale, Myrkwood, &c., are conventional heroic place-names. It was popular at a very early date in England, and is probably a Pan-Germanic legend. The Sigurd and Hild stories, on the contrary, are both, in all versions, localised on the Continent, the former by the Rhine, the latter in Friesland or Jutland; both, therefore, in Low German country, whence they must have spread to the other Germanic lands. To England they were doubtless carried by the Low German invaders of the sixth century. On the question of their passage to the North there are wide differences of opinion. Most scholars agree that there was an earlier and a later passage, the first taking Hild, Ermanric, and the Volsung story; the second, about the twelfth or thirteenth century, the Volsungs again, with perhaps Dietrich and Attila. But there is much disagreement as to the date of the first transmission. Müllenhoff[33] put it as early as 600; Konrad Maurer, in the ninth and tenth centuries; while Dr. Golther is of opinion that the Volsung story

---

[33]Müllenhoff's views are given in the *Zeitschrift für deutsches Altertum*, vol. x.; Maurer's in the *Zeitschrift für deutsche Philologie*, vol. ii. For Golther's views on the Volsung cycle see *Germania*, 33.

passed first to the vikings in France, and then westward over Ireland to Iceland; therefore also not before the ninth century. Such evidence as is afforded by the very slight English references makes it probable that the Scandinavians had the tales later than the English, a view supported by the more highly developed form of the Norse version, and, in the case of the Volsung cycle, its greater likeness to the Continental German. The earliest Norse references which can be approximately dated are in the Skald Bragi (first half of the ninth century), who knew all three stories: the Hild and Ermanric tales he gives in outline; his only reference to the Volsungs is a kenning, "the Volsungs' drink," for serpent. With the possible exception of the Anglo-Saxon fragments, the Edda preserves on the whole the purest versions of those stories which are common to all, though, as might be expected, the Continental sources sometimes show greater originality in isolated details. These German sources have entangled the different cycles into one involved mass; but in the Norse the extraneous elements are easily detached.

The motives of heroic tales are limited in number and more or less common to different races. Heroic cycles differ as a rule merely in their choice or combination of incidents, not in the nature of their material. The origin of these heroic motives may generally be found in primitive custom or conditions of life, seized by an imaginative people and woven into legend; sometimes linked to the name of some dead tribal hero, just as the poets of a later date wound the same traditions in still-varying combinations round the names of Gretti Asmundarson and Gold-Thori; though often the hero is, like the Gods, born of the myth. In the latter case, the story is pure myth; in the former it is legend, or a mixture of history and legend, as in the Ermanric and Dietrich tales, which have less interest for the mythologist.

The curse-bringing treasure, one of the most fruitful Germanic motives, probably has its origin in the custom of burying a dead man's possessions with him. In the *Waterdale Saga*, Ketil Raum, a viking of the eighth and early ninth centuries, reproaches his son Thorstein as a degenerate, in that he expects to inherit his father's wealth, instead of winning fortune for himself: "It used to be the custom with kings and earls, men of our kind, that they won for themselves fortune and fame; wealth was not counted as a heritage, nor would sons inherit from their fathers, but rather lay their possessions in the howe with them." It is easy to see that when this custom came into conflict with the son's natural desire to inherit, the sacrosanctity of the dead man's treasure and of his burial-mound would be their only protection against violation. The fear of the consequences of breaking the custom took form in the myth of the curse, as in the sword of Angantyr and the Nibelungs' hoard; while the dangers attending the violation of the howe were personified in the dragon-guardian. In *Gold-Thori's Saga*, the dead berserks whose howe Thori enters, are found guarding their treasure in the shape of dragons; while Thori himself is said to have turned into a dragon after death.[34]

---

[34] See also Hartland, *Science of Fairy-Tales*.
The eating of the dragon's heart may possibly be a survival of the custom of eating a slain enemy's heart to obtain courage, of which Dr. Frazer gives examples in the *Golden Bough*.

Marriage with alien wives[35], which in the case of the Mastermaid story has been postulated as means of transmission and as the one possible explanation of its nearly universal diffusion, may perhaps with more simplicity be assumed as the common basis in custom for independently arising myths of this type. The attempts of the bride's kindred to prevent the marriage, and of the bridegroom's to undo it, would be natural incidents in such a story, and the magic powers employed by and against the bride would be the mythical representatives of the mutually unfamiliar customs of alien tribes. This theory at least offers a credible explanation of the hero's temporary oblivion of or unfaithfulness to his protectress, after their successful escape together.

In the Valkyrie-brides, Brynhild and Sigrun, with their double attributes of fighting and wisdom, there is an evident connexion with the Germanic type of woman preserved in the allusions of Cæsar and Tacitus, which reaches its highest development in the heroines of the Edda. Any mythical or ideal conception of womanhood combines the two primitive instincts, love and fighting, even though the woman may be only the innocent cause of strife, or its passive prize. The peculiarity of the Germanic representation is that the woman is never passive, but is herself the incarnation of both instincts. Even if she is not a Valkyrie, nor taking part herself in the fight, she is ready, like the wives of the Cimbri, to drive the men back to the battle from which they have escaped. Hild and Hervör are at one extreme: war is their spiritual life. Love is in Hild nothing more than instinct; in

---

[35]For the theory of alien wives as a means of transmission, see Lang, *Custom and Myth* (London, 1893).

Hervör it is not even that: she would desire nothing from marriage beyond a son to inherit the sword. At the other extreme is Sigrun, who has the warlike instinct, but is spiritually a lover as completely and essentially as Isolde or Juliet. The interest in Signy lies in the way in which she sacrifices what are usually considered the strongest feminine instincts, without, however, by any means abandoning them, to her uncompromising revenge and pride of race. Her pride in her son seems to include something of both trains of feeling; and she dies with the husband she detests, simply because he is her husband. Brynhild, lastly, is a highly modern type, as independent in love as in war. It is impossible to imagine Sigrun, or Wagner's Sieglinde, taking her revenge on a faithless lover; from no lack of spirit, but simply because revenge would have given no comfort to either. To Brynhild it is not only a distinct relief, but the only endurable end; she can forgive when she is avenged.[36]

The other motives of these stories may be briefly enumerated. The burning of Brynhild and Signy, and Sigrun's entrance into the howe, are mythical reminiscences of widow-burial. The "sister's son" is preserved in the Sigmund and Sinfjötli tale, which also has a trace of animism in the werwolf episode. The common swanmaid[37] motive occurs in two, the Völund story and the legend of Helgi and Kara;

---

[36]See Mr. Gummere's article in the *English Miscellany*; and Professor Rhys' Presidential Address to the Anthropological Section of the British Association, 1900. The double relationship between Sigmund and Sinfjötli (not uncommon in heroic tales; compare Conchobhar and Cuchulainn, Arthur and Mordred) seems in this case due to the same cause as the custom which prevailed in the dynasty of the Ptolemies, where the king often married his sister, that his heir might be of the pure royal blood.

[37]See Hartland, *Science of Fairy-Tales*.

while the first Helgi tale suggests the Levirate in the proposed marriage of Svava to her husband's brother. The waverlowe[38] of the Volsung myth may be traced back to the midsummer fires; the wooing of Brynhild by Sigurd's crossing the fire would thus, like the similar bridal of Menglad and Svipdag and the winning of Gerd for Frey, be based on the marriages which formed a part of agricultural rites.

---

[38]Dr. Frazer (*Golden Bough*) gives instances of ritual marriages connected with the midsummer fires. For *Svipdag and Menglad*, see Study No. 12 of this series. If Rydberg, as seems very probable, is right in identifying Menglad and Svipdag with Freyja and the mortal lover who wins her and whom she afterwards loses, the story would be a parallel to those of Venus and Adonis, Ishtar and Tammuz, &c., which Frazer derives from the ritual marriage of human sacrifices to the Goddess of fertility. The reason given in the Edda for Brynhild's sleep, and her connexion with Odin, are secondary, arising from the Valhalla myth.

III

Bibliography

I. Study in the Original.

(1) *Poetic Edda.*—The classic edition, and on the whole the best, is Professor Bugge's (Christiania, 1867); the smaller editions of Hildebrand (*Die Lieder der Aelteren Edda*, Paderborn, 1876), and Finnur Jónsson (*Eddalieder*, Halle, 1888-90) are also good; the latter is in two parts, *Göttersage* and *Heldensage*. The poems may also be found in the first volume of Vigfusson and Powell's *Corpus Poeticum Boreale* (Oxford, 1883), accompanied by translations; but in many cases they are cut up and rearranged, and they suffer metrically from the system adopted of printing two short lines as one long one, with no dividing point. There is an excellent palaeographic edition of the *Codex Regius of the Elder Edda*, by Wimmer and Finnur Jónsson (Copenhagen, 1891), with photographic reproductions interleaved with a literal transcription.

(2) *Snorra Edda.*—The most recent edition of the whole is Dr. Finnur Jónsson's (Copenhagen, 1875). There is a useful edition of the mythological portions *(i.e., Gylfaginning, Bragaraedur,* and the narrative parts of *Skaldskaparmal)* by Ernst Wilken (*Die Prosäische Edda*, Paderborn, 1878).

(3) *Dictionaries and Grammars.*—For the study of the Poetic Edda, Gering's *Glossar zu den Liedern der Edda* (Paderborn, 1896) will be found most useful; it is complete Page 47and trustworthy, and in small compass. A similar service has been performed for *Snorra Edda* in Wilken's *Glossar* (Paderborn, 1883), which forms a second volume

to his edition, mentioned above. Both are, of course, in German. The only English dictionary is the lexicon of Cleasby and Vigfusson (Oxford).

Of Grammars, the best are German; those of Noreen (*Altnordische Grammatik*, Halle, 1892), of which there is an abbreviated edition, and Kahle (*Altisländisches Elementarbuch*, Heidelberg, 1896) being better suited for advanced students; the English grammars included in Vigfusson and Powell's *Icelandic Reader* (Oxford) and Sweet's *Icelandic Primer* (Oxford) are more elementary, and therefore hardly adequate for the study of the verse literature.

II. Translations.

There are English translations of the Elder Edda by Anderson (Chicago, 1879) and Thorpe (1866), as well as the translations in the *Corpus Poeticum*, which are, of course, liable to the same objection as the text. The most accurate German translation is Gering's (Leipzig, 1893); in Simrock's (*Aeltere und Jüngere Edda*, Stuttgart, 1882), the translations of the verse Edda are based on an uncritical text. Snorra Edda was translated into English by Dasent (Stockholm, 1842); also by Anderson (Chicago, 1880).

III. Modern Authorities.

To the works on Northern mythology mentioned below in the note on the Baldr theories, must be added Dr. Rydberg's *Teutonic Mythology* (English version by R.B. Anderson, London, 1889), which devotes special attention to Saxo.

Ramón Bau

Paganism as a *Weltanschauung*
Ramón Bau

To speak of paganism is to speak of one of those words that may mean almost anything, even more so among comrades pursuing "alternative" ways. The outcome of this misunderstanding of the essence of paganism, converts it from a sort of Viking mystique to a warrior's spirituality, when not just as a neurotic sect seeking a nostalgic return to pre-History. Well now, paganism is so much more than this, surpassing these facets by far.

Paganism is not a return to the past

The following definition is one of the more classical considerations based in historical reference, even though not quite right: *"we denominate paganism as a determined spiritual vision that existed in pre-Christian Europe still practiced until this very day by some of the heirs of the several Indo-European peoples"*.

In reality today "paganism" is very distinct from the "pre-Christian" religions. It was full of superstitions and practices nowadays totally abandoned, of Gods and customs that already in their time were only a scarce ordained sum of beliefs and customs that had already lost their profound and original signification.

In their "plebeian" environment Pre-Christian religions were but a mix of an enormous amount of superstitions and the traditional sources of ethnic spirituality, having generated several religious forms more inclined to the superstitious gibberish than to preserve their

Paganism as a Weltanschauung

"pagan" essence. It's not by believing in the cosmologies or in the legends - pagan Gods, that we shall be able to cast light into present-day "paganism".

On other hand, even though all of these pre-Christian religions may have common values, these are hidden behind the confused and enormous tangle of differences between each religious group. Celts, Germans, Greeks, Hindus, Sumerians, Hittites, Tartessians or Iberians, to give some examples, were much more diffuse, confused and complicated and we must consider this if we are to nowadays to address the pre-Christian religions in such a way that a "spiritual vision" becomes accessible.

As de Benoist rightly said in "*On Being a Pagan*"[39]:

"*First of all, Paganism is not a 'return to the past'; contrary to what Alain Gerard Slam stated (Lire, April 1980). It does not manifest the wish to return to a whatever lost paradise (a theme more akin to Judeo-Christianity) and even less, contrary to what Catherine Chalier (Les nouveaux cahiers, 1979) baseless states to a 'pure origin'.*"

This "refusal to return to the past" does not imply that we are to forget the examples of Themistocles, Cato, Solon, Scipio and Cincinnatus, for instance, thus recuperating not only the concept of the "saint" but of the "hero" as well, detaching ourselves from the "politically vote" category that nowadays presents itself as a democratic "example" of a human.

---

[39] BENOIST, Alain de; *Cómo se Puede ser Pagano?*, Ediciones Nueva Republica, Barcelona, 2004. English edition: *On Being a Pagan*, Ultra, 2005. French edition: *Comment peut-on êtrepaïen?*, Avatar Editions, 2009 (latest edition, the original dates back to 1981).

Paganism has no Church

This return to the past has driven many pagans to assume sectarian positions, sometimes very ridiculous.

"Neo-paganism, if neo-paganism indeed exists, is not the sectarian phenomenon that both its adversaries and its groups and circles - generally well minded, sometimes awkward, frequently laughable and generally at the fringe - imagine it to be"

I would say that paganism is an answer to a present day decadent world, which is based upon values, not in the imitation of a historical "epoch" or in the resuscitating of some archaic religions.

Nothing is less attractive to me than those mimed rites from both pre-historical paganism and an "ill transcribed Christianism", that assumes ritual forms aiming to constitute Christianity's equivalent or counterpart rites: the concept of a "Church" and a "ritual" of paganism is an absurdity.

A pagan has no Church, better still; his Church is his community, his caste, his own struggle to assure his communal survival. The pagan Church is the racial and natural community, in its nature and in its struggle to uplift and uphold that same community and its natural environment. In some way "the Political", with capital letters, is the pagan "Church".

To the pagan the action of emulating the Hero- the superior individual free from egotism and hate, from vice degradation and from that "humble" decadence of the impotent –has its origins in his community, the first circle of nature that surrounds him, in some way the "clan" is his Church or struggle community, a struggle not insomuch in a physical or warlike sense, rather ethical and experiential.

To create a "Church" is a sign of having parted with the natural community, creating a new "artificial community" that separates and breaks away from nature. This is why in the monolatrous religions the "Church" is "universal" and "equalitarian", as it breaks away from the conception of the natural community. And by that reason they are "anti-racist", for a Church of "equals before God" cannot grasp the concept of nature and natural community, it rather deals with "believers", "sons of God" instead of "sons of nature".

In that sense the ensemble of the "communitarian" pagan structure makes no sense at all, it rather must be but a popular and natural community befitting the pagan, in the midst of which he is to develop his struggle.

Paganism is not a Deist polytheism, another error is to evocate paganism as a polytheism opposing the "monolatrous" (one god and one book revealed by the Deity) religion's monotheism.

Not long ago I read on a work about paganism:

"The basis of our idiosyncrasy is monotheism. To us there is a single god, supreme, creator, increated and prior to the universe. This sole pagan god does not exist in a static sense; he evolves encompassing the world and mankind in it. It is an ineffable god, unpronounceable, Alpha and Omega, beginning and end of all things.

With this monotheistic vision we intend to overthrow what until now has been denominated, and believed so by everyone, as being the first monotheistic religion: Judaism, which has its own god but not a unique one, as they accept the existence of all the other peoples' gods.

Regardless of the multitude of gods that constitute both the Celts and the Teutons Pantheon, these are more properly said demi-god, second plan spiritual entities that may change and transform the world but that are not creators."

One can also read about it in the work of Alain de Benoist:

"Julian himself, when he reestablishes the Solar Cult, goes as far as to point out that next to the physical sun, lies the sun of divine intellect, of which the luminary is but the epiphany. Diogenes Laërtius writes: 'God, intellect, faith, Zeus, are but one being, and he is still named in many other ways' (VII, 134). Maximus of Tyre (17, 5) states on his turn that the Greeks simultaneously uphold these two truths, the first one is that: 'there is only one god, king and father of all', the second one being that, 'there are several gods, sons of god, which participate in his power'."

One thing is certain, beneath the confusion of Gods and legends, the idea of a sole creator god has always been present in pre-Christian paganism, but nowadays paganism does not even have that monotheistic or polytheistic base. Today's paganism has overcome the idea of god as "personal element external to nature", and it does not need to believe in "god" as a "being" or existent entity.

Paganism is neither polytheist nor monotheist; it is agnostic in what concerns the "gods" as "existing beings" outside natural reality.

Paganism as a Weltanschauung

The "gods" vision of paganism absolutely differs from the vision of "god" upheld by the monolatrous religions.

What indeed both ancient and modern paganism radically repeal is the idea of a sacred book. There is not a book, nor a text, but a Tradition of values, a natural reality, never an immutable text bestowed by an "entity" and to which we must obey in its written literality. This certainly points out a radical detachment from the Judaic, Christian and Islamic religions.

The idea of a historical "text" in paper, immutable and set down in writing, a product of some external god- to which one must obey to the human and natural, materialized in precepts and regulations, is absolutely opposite to the pagan spirit.

Not only the historical exegesis manages to assert the unbelievability of those texts in what concerns their original authenticity, already not "divine" but rather "truly human" (there are very clear evidences of forging in the evangelical texts, in addition to that many of the so-called apocryphal gospels were considered "acceptable" for centuries. And the biblical histories, besides being infamous in so many parts of it, do not hold historically as more than legends that have a far off or even null mythical real basis. As far as Mohammed goes, his life is far from being an exemplar one in many themes), as all of these texts originate from an external environment to our Indo-European race and to its racial tradition values.

But the important thing to understand is that polytheism is not the basis of paganism, but that polytheism is a spiritual characteristic that reflects in its essence the value of difference and of life's variety. The gods are not real but mythical reflections of the diverse facets both of Man and Nature. Each god was the reflection of a strength or valor. Each god represented that variety that Man must understand and respect. Gods of each people, of each family, of each virtue, of each natural phenomenon... everything was a reflection of that esteem for diversity opposed to monotheism's tendency for identitarian genocide and uniformity.

We are not all brothers or sons of the same god, states pagan polytheism, we are humans but not all caste brothers nor equals or of the same "created race"... we are diverse, we love that diversity. And we respect all the values, each one of them, each sign of nature and of mankind, not only those that a text has consecrated as "commanded". That's why war had a god, because struggle, value, was a polytheistic virtue. And sex had a god because sex is part of nature's powers, not a sin. The gods represented the variety of life, against monotheistic uniformity.

Paganism is neither Atheism nor Deism

It's curious but in the same way that National Socialism is accused of being "rightwing" by some and of being "socialist" and "massifier" by the rightwing Traditionalists, paganism likewise is accused of "atheism" by the Christians and of "mystical deism" by the Marxist atheists and by the progressists.

Though paganism in itself does not depend upon the existence of a God, nonetheless it does not object to the believing in a Deity, either.

In his work on paganism, de Benoist states:

Paganism as a Weltanschauung

"Paganism, far from characterizing itself by a repulse of spirituality or a refusal of the sacred, consists otherwise in the choice of other spirituality, of another form of conceiving the sacred.

The sense of sacred, of spirituality, of faith, the believe in the existence of God, religion as an ideology, religion as a system and as an institution are different notions that don't necessarily entwine. They are not univocal. There are religions that have no God (as for instance Taoism); to believe in God does not necessarily imply that we are dealing with a personal God.

For paganism, God cannot be completely dissociated from the world; and it cannot be so as He is the primeval absolute cause to which the world is united to, and men are not contingent creatures to which he has given life ex-nihilo. Paganism refuses the idea of a primeval absolute creation, central to Judeo-Christian monotheism in the same way that it refuses all mechanicist epistemology."

We could summon this up by saying that paganism has no need for a personal God external to nature, of which man forms part as one more element, not as something "distinct in His essence". The miracle is nature, the cosmos, and the presence or the absence of a god is something somewhat secondary, it is a way of "expressing" our spirituality before the miracle.

Pagan spirituality is a passionate and burning admiration for the great miracle of life and of existence, for that opportunity that life presents us to be superior, to display the best and the higher in us instead of the worst and miserable: To be masters of our own fate and not slaves to our vices. The miracle of the cosmos and its beauty, together with the implacable or ruthless cycle of life and death, being that death itself is a part of that miracle, not a punishment or a step towards "another life" but a "step in this life" (another life that is presented by the religions as the "real one", like if this one were to be a farce or a punishment), a death that one has to approach with the same passion as life itself.

Pagan spirituality is therefore love to life and death, love to nature and to its vital miracle, whether it originates from a god or from which that Monod called "chance and need".

De Benoist states quite rightfully:

"In Olympus, Heraclitus says, 'the gods are immortal men, while men are mortal gods; our life is their death and our death is their life' (Frag. 62). One could not express better that between men and gods there is a difference of level, but not a radical difference in nature. The gods are made to the image of men, of which they present a sublimated representation".

This is man's sublime vision, the chance to become a god, an ideal, or to just turn out to be a miserable piece of decadent meat, those are the ones that the gods despise by their "impiety", that is to say by their turpitude.

The gods are the ideal of man, and man may become god or plebs, and this is the only thing he can attain out of this brief space in time in which the miracle of life gives him the opportunity to become something.

Paganism is to be driven, in that time lapse, to aspire to godliness, to be the hero, the one who overcomes mere pleasure, instead of being only a consumer of his egotism. To ride his Self in pursuit of the sublime or be ridden by his own egotism pursuing material pleasure, here is the dilemma for which paganism offers a personal answer, without the need for gods to command and belittle it…

Since the one that is a hero because a god has commanded him to be so is only "the slave" of his god, he has not made the decision by himself, but is only obeying his "master". More common still is he that is a hero to achieve pleasure in "another life", this one is just like the usurer that deprives himself of expenditure bearing in mind the interests that he will collect in the future!

Only the one who acts on his own will, by his own believes and desires, is capable of being a hero and to grow closer to the gods… or to fall in the waste of his egotism… this very decision is the one that sublimes or degenerates, not the commandments of "others".

What is paganism?

We have already spent plenty on this theme in the previous titles, but we need to wrap up a definition, however complex the subject may be.

I believe that a definition paganism must be made today based on a spirituality focused on the recuperation of the essential values of the Indo-European peoples, eliminating the superstitious aspects, the elements alien to our race, and above all the biblical and encyclopaedical[40], which have infected Aryan spirituality.

---

[40] After Diderot's work "L'Encyclopedie" sensed both by its detractors and supporters as being a catalyst agent for the advent of the French revolution. The 18th-century movement that it

The essential base of paganism is to seek personal enhancement through and for the advance of the community and the natural environment of which one is part of, based in some values that are intrinsic to our race and that have been hidden or degenerated through two nefarious tendencies: biblical monolatrous and materialist rationalism. Nature opposing the unreal utopia imposed by a book or by the power of profit.

The idea that "human" values are not distinct from those of nature is the basis for paganism's opposition to the monolatrous idea that nature is but a tool of the "human being as the only one that matters in the divine" (biblical vision) or that nature is an "economic asset", a mere part of the production process to be exploited for the sole and exclusive human interest (democratic vision, either Marxist or Capitalist).

Self-control and triumph over of all vices in a struggle path aiming for all that is the reflection of a "heroic" life, that's enhancement.

Pagan heroism is not a violent attitude, but an acceptance of risk and sacrifice of egotism to be able to grow closer to an ideal of heroic virtues: valor, honor, truthfulness, love towards the community, respect for nature, style, culture and art, beauty, dignity, helping those in need, compassion by the grievances of our fellow men, despise for he who sells out or allows himself to be belittled by money, justice delivered to the culprit, etc…

We are speaking of spirituality, but for the pagan this word does

---

embodied – the Encyclopedists - was based on the belief that rationalism, could find true knowledge and lead mankind to progress and happiness, thus opposing reactionary forces in church and state.

not imply something necessarily supernatural but rather that human ability to deeper submerge, sentimentally and inimically, into the innermost profound Self, escaping rationalism and penetrating in the essentially sensible, in the world of values, facing the world of interests.

Philosophically speaking, the partisans of the exclusive primacy of the logos over the mythos, from Descartes and Auguste Comte to Marx and Adorno, oppose the partisans of mythos, from Vico to Heidegger, Schopenhauer and Nietzsche as well as almost every artist until the arrival of modern barbarism…

Therefore there is no reason to mistake anti-rationalism for an anti-scientific attitude or a belittlement of reason and logic; we rather put reason at the service of Man and not Man servicing reason's utopias. I'm going to give an example. Rationalism has a tendency to invent equal men, but this is neither real nor would it be good to be so, we are not equal and it is good that we are not.

Rationalism has a liking for to speak of rights but never of duties, it is favorable to invent utopian and precious rights like the one inscribed in the [Spanish] Constitution (the right to proper housing, to a decent work and a thousand of other precious things…) that from the start are never meant to be fulfilled, whereas paganism speaks of duties and, only after having fulfilled those, rights, and when it speaks of a right it is a feasible one, not an utopia for propagandistic amusement.

Paganism is realist, not utopian. It uses reason to do combat but not to make up heavens and utopias (the Communist heaven of free proletarians is even more utopic than the hubris of the paradise promised by Mohammed).

This special valorization of the ethereal and the sensible dimension in the humane, versus the valorization of his economic, pleasurable or utilitarian aspect differentiates paganism from materialist rationalism (either Capitalist or Marxist). Meanwhile, the valorization of nature as root of Man himself and of his values separates it from utopianism and from biblical anti-naturalism and its subsequent religious consequences.

In some way Saint Francis of Assisi's "Christian paganism" that praises our "sister the moon", "our brother the wind", "our sister the earth", "our mother that sustains and nourishes us", and above all "our brother the sun" is a heretic and schismatic contradiction of Christianism (that he almost paid with the stake) in that for the Bible and the evangelical exegesis (and Islam shares this vision) all of the extra-human is but a "tool" of Man, created to his liking, having nothing to do with the "salvific" and "celestial" message of the monolatrous religion.

Compassion, injustice and paganism

"Amongst the Indo-Europeans- Jean Varenn notes - *there is continuity between the most humble of the creatures and the highest of gods. This does not imply that all of these beings are equal; quite the opposite, they form clearly separated and hierarchized groups... The norm is for each living being to fully assume his own condition or as the Veddu puts it, hisdháman: simultaneously 'statute' and 'position', that is to say his rank in the beings' hierarchic scale"*[41]

---

[41] *Dictionnaire des Mythologies*, Flammarion, 1980, p. 45

Paganism as a Weltanschauung

At first sight it may seem that paganism proclaims the acceptance of oppressions and injustice based in the "acceptance of one's position". That is not, absolutely, the meaning of the community's social hierarchy with paganism. Other than that, paganism establishes that each one, whenever placed in his just position, should be happy with his work and condition. This is always the necessary position in the community thus possessing the maximal importance for each individual, insofar that the street cleaner should not feel (as it does in Capitalism) despised when compared to the engineer, nor should he hate (as in Marxism) the head of a company. All of this, in the assumption that we are living in a just system in which each one receives accordingly to his work and responsibility, different but not abusively distinct.

In paganism the success of human live does not resides in the office held but in the human value of each one.

Nevertheless one of paganism's principles is the struggle against injustice; therefore all oppression or ill treatment must be fought off, and not "accepted".

Following this trend, the pagan and Indo-European peoples are the ones in which women have received better treatment when compared to peoples of other races or those subdued to the monolatrous religions.

And also still better than in the encyclopaedical and Marxist societies, where a woman has the right to be a prostitute but not a mother of five desired children by lack of means, with the right to work as a man but not to be with her offspring in the childhood years when it would be more appropriate for their mother to accompany them. Paganism puts natural values before the economic ones, and for that it proposes a respected and valued women society in comparison to the "masculinized" degraded women, resembling "men".

Another one of the great misunderstandings on paganism is its assimilation to a harsh, cruel, uncompassionate society, disdaining the weak and the helpless. This idea is based upon two errors:

- Assigning paganism to the customs of the primitive years, where customs were cruel and life was often harsh. Christians have assimilated paganism to the Romans of the imperial era that killed or tortured, to the Spartans that threw the feeble children into the cliffs, and to Vikings that slaughtered cities and enslaved women and children.

- The repugnant custom of the democrats to present the culprit as feeble, the scoundrel as someone deprived, the opportunist as oppressed, the imbecile as handicapped. Paganism has no compassion regarding the culprit, nor with the scoundrel, the despicable opportunist or the free willing imbecile. But authentic paganism has nothing to do with brutality or cruelty, which is a corruption of Man, a lack of sensibility. As it is a lack of value the acceptance of the culprits blackmailing for to reclaim aid and pity by their former stupidity and evil doing.

Compassion regarding the innocent and the ill-treated justice and force against those who by their own wickedness and stupidity are the laborers of their own disgrace.

Struggle, action and movement

Life means movement and dynamism, that being so there is no escaping it. The static contemplation of the world's injustices or wickedness is not inherent to paganism.

It is appropriate to say of paganism that it is a dynamic pessimism, a simultaneously tragic and accepted vision of life in which one struggles regardless of hope, struggling not for victory but by the ethical need to do so.

One can read on paganism:

"...the three armed solar symbol, the triskele, derived from the wheel and, as such, akin with the also ancient venerable swastika, both present in all the Indo-European peoples.

'Change is the only thing that never changes in the world'. From this comes our detachment for the material and our comprehension of how transient life is, expressed by the absence of great permanent settlements, of impressive physical stone temples or of the simple need in leaving note of one's own existence, after one's dead, other than familiar memory.

This evolution-involution is the eternal becoming that rules the laws of cosmos and of all its essence. There is no life without death, nor death without life, or day without night, nor night without day. We therefore base our notion of the absolute divine, in an entity in constant becoming. The whole is subdued to a dynamic process, of continual creation, of evolution, whose symbols are made known with the passing of time".

To the pagan there is no heaven awaiting him, rather than that, his own struggle and value is his heaven, his reward, to know that one has fulfilled his heroic task is the biggest reward that a pagan may expect. The pagan does not ask a reward for being heroic, to live up to his own values, he does not want heavens nor prizes or applauses from external gods; it is his own honor that rewards him. The one who has the need of a reward to be honorable is already a man without honor.

This vision of nature shows us the dynamic and hazardous reality of life. Nothing in nature is eternal, nothing is foreseen; nothing is safe. The same happens in life and history. "The way is paved by the struggle", there is no promised victories, nor science that ensures the success of whatever idea, and there is no "end of history" either. Man himself, and the Earth, have their days numbered, perhaps in a few million years, but no more. Everything shall pass, and empires have always lasted less than a thousand years.

For this paganism does not believe in cycles or in a linear history, it does not believe that history is already defined, reality is made at every moment of the struggle.

"The old must die for the new to arrive. Annihilation awaits us but one should know how to educate ourselves in the quiet acceptance of fate. We must be aware of what awaits us but without refusing neither joy nor singing. The spirit must not become retracted."

The concept of the pagan world on the "eternal becoming" does not mean that everything returns but that everything changes. The whole is submitted to a dynamical process, of continuous creation.

There are pagans that believe in a god and in the immortality of the soul, in reincarnation, all of it in a diffused form, as a personal creed, without "other world" theology, rather as a personal belief.

Personally I believe that any such creed in this sense is risky as it is scarcely based. Agnosticism is not the denial of something but the impossibility of knowing about something. I do not know if there is anything after death, but based on what life tells me there are no motives to undoubtedly believe in something. And besides that, one's conduct should not in any way vary regardless of the existence or absence of "another world". Man's conduct should never be dictated according to "another life", of rewards, punishments or future hopes, rather by the mandate of honor and will of power to carry out, or not, what is expected from us in that path of enhancement that one should chart.

Mystique and love in paganism

If paganism were to be but an idea, it would be worthless to continue to speak about it. It is precisely because it does not believe in the primacy of the logos over feeling, that paganism is above all a state of mind, a sensible way of approaching life and the individual. One feels more like a pagan than he thinks like a pagan.

The pagan feels a profound love for nature, for cosmos and the existence, for death itself and for all that is noble and simple… we feel like a part of nature and we love what we are, if we know how to be noble we are not to desire "another life" but this one carried out nobly and simply. Therefore without love, but a love to the noble and natural, not to all, paganism has no sense.

Out of that feeling of belonging to nature, of this love to life and to nobility - when it is sublimated and one arrives to be deeply rooted in it - arises the pagan mystique, which is but a spiritual state of internal sublimation of that love for nature. That mystique takes form in deeds and facts as holding meetings in the woods or reading poetry around a bonfire in a mountain summit, feeling in contact with what one truly is, nature in its virginal and primeval state. Or getting in touch with those human works that remind us of times when Man was closer to nature. This pagan mystique does not correspond to a copy of pre-Christian times, but rather to an approach to some ideals.

At last, we may say, that to be a pagan is a form of being a National Socialist, not the only way, but one among them.

www.ingramcontent.com/pod-product-compliance
Lightning Source LLC
Chambersburg PA
CBHW031407040426
42444CB00005B/453